THE ART OF
SERVANT
LEADERSHIP
II

How You Get Results Is More Important
Than the Results Themselves

ART BARTER

The Art of Servant Leadership II:
How You Get Results Is More Important Than the Results Themselves

Published by Wheatmark®
2030 East Speedway Boulevard, Suite 106
Tucson, Arizona 85719 USA
www.wheatmark.com

ISBN: 978-1-62787-513-4 (paperback)
ISBN: 978-1-62787-514-1 (hardcover)
ISBN: 978-1-62787-515-8 (ebook)
LCCN: 2018931157

rev012018

Table of Contents

Foreword

The Art of Servant Leadership II is about how leaders can shape a servant-led culture in which people achieve extraordinary results. Art Barter, CEO of Datron World Communications and founder of the Servant Leadership Institute, has written an extraordinary book. It is Art's story, his story of personal growth as a leader and his story of the transformation of a "command and control" organization that was losing money into a profitable, servant led company. This story will inspire you and it will equip you with the knowledge and tools that can otherwise take a lifetime to learn.

Art invites you to be a game changer in how you influence and impact your world. As Art's story unfolds, you will learn the grand design and the specific tactics required to change people's hearts, mindsets, and behaviors.

I met Art at the end of 2004, just as he had completed the purchase of Datron from Titan Corporation. He wasn't in his office, and I found him on the manufacturing floor in a work coat, organizing parts on a shelf. That is Art. He is as concerned about the details as he is about the great vision and concepts that make organizations work. He told me then "I want servant leadership to be the DNA of Datron." As a consultant, trainer, and coach I have worked with CEO's over three decades, yet I have never met a CEO who exemplifies such caring and commitment for people and such perseverance for bold goals *and* the detailed actions of execution.

Art is also willing do the hardest work of all, the work on

himself. This is the gift he gives to you—the reality of what it takes to lead and change yourself and your company. I encourage you to take notes as you read this book because each chapter will arm you with concepts and tools that you can adapt to your own organization. The art and practice of servant leadership will change your life. It changed mine.

Central to this guide are the nine behaviors that are the foundation for creating a servant led organization, a powerful strategy for individual and organizational change. These nine behaviors are a model for living. When we live these behaviors in small and large actions every day, we are at our best and we bring out the best in others. If you have coached or mentored successfully, you were undoubtedly coaching to one or more of the nine behaviors.

You will connect with each of the challenges Art experienced over more than a decade of building a servant-led culture. He will describe how he learned to let go and get out of the way so others could learn and grow as leaders. And you will understand why he had to step back in when Datron was experiencing "culture drift."

The measurement of success for a servant leader is do those you serve grow? Are they better off because they have come in contact with you? This book is your field guide to growing individuals while you grow your organization. "Time," Art says, "is your most valuable asset," and he encourages his managers to have the discipline to invest time in their people.

You will be surprised that one of the most effective strategies to help leaders transform is to put them into a safe environment with a small group of their peers. Let them set their own agenda so they can openly discuss their challenges. They will each grow at their own rate, but that growth is accelerated by their peers. Art will also encourage you to bring in the great leadership teachers of our time. These teachers have the wisdom to engage your team's spouses and partners, people who are often forgotten in the equation of how we grow leaders.

Art is more concerned with how we get results than the

results themselves. Living by this maxim, he has led Datron to unprecedented financial success, as well as helped Datron through and out of hard times. This story is as real as it gets, and Art is frank about the tension of needing to achieve business results while you and your people are in the process of learning how to be leaders that serve others.

The task of being a servant leader requires that you know yourself: your history, your life stories, and how they have shaped your development as a leader. It means knowing your character, what you stand for, and knowing where you stand. It is a lifelong process. It is the exploration of your creative expression in life. It is your life's work and the hardest work you will ever do. Make no mistake, servant leadership is not easy, but it is what our world needs—the commitment to unite for the greater good, a world in which we help others succeed.

Jeanne McGuire
Lafayette, California
January 2018

Acknowledgments

I would like to thank the team at the Servant Leadership Institute for their endless patience and support in developing and advising on this book project. They are a great team of servant leaders who inspired and equipped me throughout this project. I especially want to thank the following people:

Lisa Courtemanche, my executive assistant, who has run my life for the past four years. Thank you for your servant's heart and your desire to help me be the best I can be.

Nonie Jobe, my writer and editor, our first project together. You have blessed me with your desire for my voice to be heard in my writings and for this I am eternally grateful.

The leadership team at Datron World Communications, which participated, witnessed, and survived my own transformation. You continue to inspire and equip me each and every day by your desire to get better in serving others, for making a positive difference in the lives around you, and for putting others first in your lives. Thank you for acknowledging that no one is perfect and for the grace you extend to me when my old power leader behaviors come out.

The team at Wheatmark, who have recognized that we have a calling in serving others. Your input on this project and final help in getting this over the finish line for our annual leadership conference is greatly appreciated by the entire team at the Institute.

My family—Lori, my wife and best friend, and Jennifer and Chris, who were on the front lines of my transformation.

You continue to inspire me to be a better father and husband each and every day. Your support throughout the years after the purchase of Datron in 2004 has been amazing. But most importantly, thank you for your unconditional love during those tough years before I realized I needed to change. I love you!!

Introduction

Servant leadership is much more than just another leadership style. It's the essence of an organization's substance and character, coming from the heart of its leaders and providing the highest value for those it serves. Servant leaders, like all leaders, come in all shapes and sizes and from all levels of education and experience. They are true leaders in every sense of the word. But the trait that sets them—and the impact they have on the world—far apart from the norm is that they lead from the heart.

That fundamental characteristic of a servant leader—one who leads with a servant's heart first and foremost—is the driving force behind the extraordinary results experienced by most servant-led organizations. The goal of servant leaders is to inspire and equip those they influence to be the best they can be. By leading with this focus, they grant the real power to make an organization great to the employees within, who become committed and engaged like never before. The myth that servant leadership is soft and not demanding enough to get the results needed in today's markets couldn't be further from the truth. When leaders overlay their education, experience, and mindset with their hearts, I believe they accomplish one of the most valuable and transformational behaviors of a leader—one that brings astonishing results while helping others grow.

Many believe that the academic side of servant leadership can create the transformation required for serving others first.

Others say that hearing the stories of those whose lives and mindset have been impacted by servant leadership—the heart behind it—is what drives the transformation of a leader. I can tell you from personal experience that the best methodology encompasses both approaches, and that neither can stand alone to drive leaders to change their ways and create a mindset of serving.

Many of our clients in the Servant Leadership Institute come to us because they've seen how we have taken the principles of servant leadership and implemented them in our radio company, Datron World Communications, Inc. In 2004 my wife Lori and I decided to purchase Datron World Communications, Inc. from the Titan Corporation. Up to that point, neither of us had ever owned a business. Both of our careers had been in manufacturing, hers in the operations side and mine in the finance and management side. When we purchased Datron, we were sure of one thing: we did not want to run our company with traditional leadership models that focused on results only, power to those in charge, and financial success to the sacred few at the top of the organizational chart. We wanted to run the company as a servant-led organization.

There was only one problem: we knew *nothing* about running a company of this size. All we had was our faith and a desire to be obedient to what our faith taught us. We are forever grateful that in 2003—just the year before—Ken Blanchard had spoken at our church, New Venture Christian Fellowship, and had challenged us to take the tenets of our faith and put them to work in the way we lead others. In other words, he challenged us to be servant leaders. Little did we know that the timing was providential.

I had been a fan of Ken Blanchard for many years prior to meeting him in 2003. I had read most of his books, and particularly his *One Minute Manager*, which I had read from cover to cover many times. But I confess that I had never purposely considered putting others first in *all* I did in life until that first meeting with Ken. Since that time, he has become a wonderful supporter of the Servant Leadership Institute, an incredible mentor, and great personal friend.

So our first application of servant leadership in our lives was when Ken got the ball rolling in 2003. Then we purchased Datron in November of 2004 and suddenly found ourselves in the role of business owners and leaders of a company. In all honesty, we had no idea what we were doing or what our plan was for the first year. At the time of the purchase, Datron was generating about $10 million in annual revenue and was losing money. I remember telling Lori that I was sure we could turn the company around so that it could be a profitable $20-million company. I had no idea how limiting my own mindset was at the time.

Prior to Titan's purchase of Datron in 2001, the company had made a profit and had been in a positive cash flow position for fifteen consecutive years. The challenge arose when its customers in developing countries began placing inconsistent orders. Some quarters would see $2 million in revenue, while others would see $5 million. Unfortunately, showing quarterly profits along with growth in revenue was expected by the shareholders of a public company, and that became a challenge for Datron. When we bought it and made it a private company, it changed that landscape; but the inconsistency of our markets created interesting difficulties from a cash-flow standpoint.

We determined to make servant leadership the key ingredient of our mindset, and that allowed us to manage our challenges in a different way. First we created a purpose that said we would positively impact the lives of others, today and in the future. Then we reinforced that purpose by sharing with our employees on a regular basis communications we received from our customers that described the impact our products were having on them and the security of their countries. By consistently communicating that purpose over and over, along with the impact we were having, we were successful in transforming our mindset into one that served first. Our purpose, supported by values that put our families first, created a driving force in all that we do.

We purposefully did not create any plans that set a growth target for the business, choosing instead to allow our customers to determine our growth. We believed that if we served our customers well, they would return for products and services over and over again. As we served them, they would decide with their checkbooks how fast we would grow. The results were phenomenal—far beyond any growth target we could have conceived in the beginning.

In this book we offer a case study in transforming a company into a servant-led organization. It starts with individual leaders who are willing to begin the inward journey of transformation of heart and soul. They allow the servant leadership behaviors to renovate their hearts, and ultimately this transfers into their hands of service. When their teams see the radical transformation of their leaders, they are inspired to start their own inward journey toward servant leadership, which finally leads to a servant-led organization.

That may sound a bit sentimental or trite to you, and you may think it's an unrealistic model for the competitive corporate world. However, *putting others first in all you do has a way of realigning your focus with your purpose in life and clarifying your principles for living your purpose on a day-to-day basis.* You will discover a new way of thinking—a new mindset—about results and about your responsibility to treat everyone with dignity and respect. At Datron we do not shy away from the need to be financially successful in our business. We don't shy away from setting and achieving goals that stretch our imagination. But we do focus *first* on the importance of obtaining those results in a way that will serve the best interest of everyone in accordance with our values.

Early in our success I was told that when we reached a revenue level of around $50 million, the management team would need to be upgraded to one with experience in running that size company. When we received a record order in 2007 I told my team to add a few more zeros to our revenue plan, but that we could do this. From an excellent book called *Mindset*, by Carol Dweck, we had learned that we could reset our internal monologue, or mindset, to a positive, growth-oriented mindset that would allow us to handle this new level of growth. So we changed our mindset to pursue the goal of serving our customer by meeting this need, which meant we needed to up our game. We would still plan our procurement, buy the materials to support that plan, expand the labor force to build the product, and deliver the completed product to the customer by the date requested. We knew how to accomplish all of this; we just had to change our mindset to accommodate a higher volume of activity. Servant leadership gave us the foundation to grow our business substantially with just the normal added expense of additional labor. In other words, by following the principles of servant leadership, we were able as a committed and engaged team to create a growth mindset and far exceed our normal production with basically what we already had. In today's corporate world, that's called increased productivity.

Servant leadership is not a designed program, nor is it the latest fad in management. Servant leadership is a way of life that has a deep impact on those you serve and influence. Implementing servant leadership is not for the faint of heart. It is a very rewarding journey that requires a commitment to behaviors and results at a very high level. Few will take the journey with you, but many will be impacted by your influence.

Early in my career I dreamed of running a division for a large public corporation. The dream included retiring when I was in my forties with a home on the bay in Newport Beach, California, with my yacht docked in my back yard. Interestingly, no one in leadership ever took the time to ask me about my dreams, much less teach me how to get there or even warn me about the sacrifices involved in making my dreams a reality. And I have to say that nowhere in my dreams did I see buying a public company, taking it private, and running it under a new set of beliefs and a new mindset. It wasn't until I was in my fifties that I even learned the difference between having significance and having success. Success is focused on yourself—climbing the corporate ladder, driving a company car, and traveling around the world in first class. Significance is all about others—using the influence that has been gifted to you to make a difference in the lives of other people.

Early in 2015 we released a book titled *Farmer Able*, a fable about a farmer whose challenges forced him to learn a new way of living, serving others. The story shows how Farmer Able implemented servant leadership in his life and on the farm; but most importantly it shows how servant leadership impacted his relationship with his wife Patience and his daughter Sunny.

The joy that servant leadership will bring to those in your world will more than offset any misgivings you may have about starting this journey. Combine your education, experience, and desire for change to start the journey that will transform your life and the lives of those around you. Join the movement of new leaders—those that lead with their hearts and discover no limits.

Prologue

I consider myself a witness. I've been here since 1977. And now I've been asked to tell you about it: the many goings on here at Datron World Communications. It's an old story that began when the hourglass of time turned over in 1971, the year the company was founded.

Some call me CEO or president, others call me owner, but those that know me the best call me Art. They have seen me in various forms and emotions over time. What they haven't seen is what I've seen; not just the happenings, but also the manner of them. Many a word, many a joy and even many a tear have passed by me and I've taken them all in. I collect the memories like they were yesterday; precious and not to be forgotten, good or bad.

Power leader I am, transformed by experiences and people to see the light of a new way of leading. I have a role to play today, one that focuses on service above self. As a servant leader my role is to pour my life into others. In doing so, I experience the transformative effect on my life when those around me grow to their own fullest potential. I'm a witness to what can be accomplished by individuals and organizations when leaders decide to serve first. In November 2004, I shared with employees that at times opportunity is missed because it comes dressed in overalls and requires a lot of hard work. I committed myself then to make all we could out of the opportunity put in front of us called Datron.

I'm a witness to the hard work. I applaud those that joined

me in transforming the world of Datron into a servant led organization. I'm in awe of the transformation that took place in the lives around me. I'm thankful for the grace extended by the Datron family that allowed me time to learn and transform my behaviors into those of a servant leader. I'm thankful to God for allowing me to witness this journey.

And what I've beheld at Datron has a certain wisdom to it—a truth of sorts, that service to others above oneself is surely worth the journey. My life has been changed for good. Take the journey and become a witness along with me.

1

Create and Communicate

"The best way to find yourself is to lose
yourself in the service of others."

—Mahatma Gandhi

Servant leadership is a mindset, and transformation from one mindset to another only occurs through consistent communication that creates an understanding about the value that mindset brings. Communication, then, is a primary tool of servant leaders.

We live in a world where many people don't know who they are, what their purpose is, or how they fit into this thing called life. As children grow up in the turmoil and chaos that too often define our culture, their confusion about life manifests in the choices they make and the masks they wear over the span of their lifetimes. As we go about the business of inspiring and equipping people to be the best they can be, our first job is to help them find purpose. As we help them find and understand their own purpose, we equip them to wholeheartedly embrace the purpose of the families and organizations they serve, and the world is made a better place.

Who Are You, and What Do You Stand For?

What about you? You are unique, and you've been given certain gifts and talents to share with the world. Do you know what they are? What is your passion? What makes you smile as you get up in the morning and face the day? Do you know your mission and purpose?

In a discussion about leadership with an executive team from another company earlier this year, I heard about a study they had done with hospice nurses, asking them this question: "What do most people talk about in the last season of their lives?" Many of the hospice nurses said the biggest thing people struggle with at the end of their lives is that they wish they had lived the life of the person they had inside of them, and not the person they thought they had to be. They felt they had to be someone else to be accepted, so they gave up their identity and their purpose.

We all have to make a living, and we all have those things that we are passionate about. Sometimes, if we are really fortunate, those two things come together and we're able to get paid for fulfilling our passion, or we get to work in a company whose mission and purpose we can be passionate about. When the values of the company we work for match our values as individuals, that's when we're happy to go to work, take pleasure in what we're doing, enjoy the people we work with, and enthusiastically embrace our opportunity to make a difference. And when an organization has a team full of happy people, it makes life easier for everyone. The organization performs well, its people are rewarded, and together they make a massive impact on the world around them.

On the other end of the spectrum, we see what happens to those who have no clue about their purpose and have no hope of ever having a meaningful life. The suicide rate continues to rise at an alarming rate especially among teens. According to Statistic Brain Research Institute, the average number of attempted teenage suicides each year is 575,000. Thankfully, the number of those who succeed is much lower (4,600 a year, or twelve a day—one out of every 125 attempted)[1], but that number is certainly nothing to boast about. One suicide is one

---

1   "Teen Suicide Statistics," Statistic Brain Research Institute, http://www.statistic-brain.com/teen-suicide-statistics (accessed 11/7/15).

too many. The point is youth are growing up so confused, with everyone trying to tell them who they think they should be, that too many of them are deciding it's better not to be alive. That's another sad statistic that bears out the fact that the overwhelming majority of people don't know who they are or what they want out of life. People are either afraid to live the life that's inside of them or they struggle to define who they really are. Either way, we as servant leaders need to help them.

There is a caveat here that we, as servant leaders, need to heed. As the world changes at lightning speed around us, we are challenged to change our thinking and enlarge our paradigm about how to help people find out who they are. We must be diligent to live by the values we say we live by, which includes inspiring and equipping those who don't fit within our boxes of social acceptability.

When Lori and I bought Datron in 2004 and were wrestling with what would be the perfect mission and purpose statement for our company, Ken Blanchard gave us some great advice: "Make your mission and purpose statement something that people understand and can latch on to." He told us stories of companies he had consulted with that had written mission and purpose statements that were three pages long! We wanted something that described what was in our hearts and that we were ready to dedicate our lives to, and this is what we came up with: "We want to be a profitable, self-sustaining communications company that positively impacts the lives of others, today and in the future."

Our purpose is to "positively impact the lives of others, today and in the future." That's certainly easy to remember and easy to talk about (especially since we're so passionate about it). Our mission, to be a "profitable and self-sustaining communications company," supports our purpose.

To us, being profitable and self-sustaining includes being debt-free. We don't believe in taking on debt to grow through acquisitions or burdening our organization with debt in any other way. As we grew the company from the $10-million level up to the $200-million level, there were times when we had to take out a line of credit with our bank; but we paid it back as soon as we could, usually within a three- to six-month period. And our mantra of being debt free precludes us from playing games with accounting systems. We don't want to have to explain, "Yes, we're losing money on paper; but we're actually making money." We keep it very simple. We have to be profitable, or we won't be able to sustain what we want to do.

Datron World Communications is a military communications company. When I speak around the country, people often ask, "How can you positively impact the lives of others when you're in a military business?" Here's a story I tell that illustrates our purpose of positively impacting the lives of others:

I started working with the police in Zimbabwe early on, after I joined Datron in the late nineties. On my first business trip to Zimbabwe I met the signals officer in the police department, and I asked him, "How can we help you?" He said, "Here's my problem. When we have presidential elections, people demonstrate in the streets. Some of those people are my friends," he said, "and some of them are even my family members. As an officer in the police department, I want to control those crowds with good communications and not with bullets." I told him we would help him do that, and we started working with him to provide the radios he needed.

After the presidential election of 2008, news articles claimed it would "go down in history as one of the most peaceful elections in Zimbabwe's history" (*New York Times*, April 18, 2008). We were elated that we had provided the communication equipment to make that happen. I called everyone in the company together, read one of the articles to them, and said, "This is why we do what we do. We save lives. That's our purpose."

Before we ship out the radios that our employees manufacture, we ask those employees, "Would you put that radio on your son's or daughter's back if he or she were going into battle?" If the answer is yes, then we ship it. If the answer is no, then it doesn't go out the door. That's how we bring out the passion of our purpose; there are men and women in the battlefield around the world who are laying down their lives to make this world a better place, and we want to help them do that with the communications equipment we manufacture.

There's an even more widespread application of our purpose. As the CEO of Datron, I deal with a lot of generals in foreign countries where we do business. We're in many nations that are in the hotspot of the world right now, and we're finding that there are a lot of good people in very difficult situations. Everywhere I go, all of the foreign generals I talk to say the same thing: they want to protect the sovereignty of their nations and provide security for their citizens. None of them want to attack other nations. They want to protect who they are and protect the individuals in their countries. The crazier the world gets, the more astounded I am at that. These military leaders are in a position to pick up the phone and send an armored tank after anyone they want to, and yet all they want to do is preserve their nations and protect their citizens, just like we do here in the US. But that's not the kind of thing we hear in the US media. I know for a fact that when the uprisings and demonstrations started in one country where we do business, their army never pulled out their weapons until outsiders started coming into their country—and when they were forced to use their weapons, they used rubber bullets instead of real ones. That's the level of integrity some of the people have who we deal with in the militaries around the world. They want peace; nobody wants war. That is why we do what we do.

We believe we have a noble purpose—one that people can really believe in. Even though our business is a military business, it's not about war—it's about saving lives. We often hire ex-military radio men who understand our products, and they love dealing with us for that very reason.

Live What You Stand For

As we carry out our own mission, purpose, and core values every day, we have to make sure we live what we stand for. And that includes the premise that if we encounter someone in a foreign nation who isn't at that level of commitment of just providing security and sovereignty, we have to make a decision whether we want to support that military. We've actually dealt with a couple of countries that were riding the fence of a good relationship with the US, and then they did some inappropriate things. In those instances we walked away because we didn't want to do business with them.

As servant leaders, you have to stand up for what's right; and by doing that you have to be willing to walk away from business. Many years ago, one of our customers in a country in the Middle East asked us to backdate some documents on a procurement process, and we said, "No, we won't do that." I told my team to get on a plane and come home. We won't backdate documents or do anything else illegal to get business. We walked away from a $6-million deal. Interestingly, eight years later that customer came back to us and asked us to take the lead on a $12-million program because of our level of integrity. They knew they could trust us. You have to live what you believe in, and you can't loosen your values just to get business. Sometimes you have to stand up and say no.

Communicate to Inspire Your Organization

Servant leaders make sure they are in front of their people all the time, reinforcing the organization's purpose. And that doesn't mean just telling them what orders are coming in and sharing the financial results. In our case, that involves telling our team about the impact they're having in a country. Whenever we travel into a country and win some business, we always come back and share in our monthly employee meetings what's going on, who we talked to, the events we were involved in, information about the customers, and what we learned about how our products will be used to help that country. That's how we inspire our people—by sharing the stories of what happens with our customers in the places we go.

In late 2016, I traveled to Morocco to sign a $20-million contract with the Ministry of Defense. It was during Ramadan; and we had been a little hesitant about going because we didn't know if we would be able to get any business done. But by being there during Ramadan, we learned much about the Muslim religion and how they observe their holy month. They fast from both food and drink during the day, from dawn until sunset. They do business for a couple of hours during the day, but most of the business is done at night. Around eight o'clock in the evening, everyone gathers in social areas. They have dinner; and then they sit around and talk for several hours, and they have community. I spent more time out on the lawn, sitting and talking with people and enjoying community than I have in a long time. I got to the point where I really looked forward to the social time each evening. We had an amazing time being there during Ramadan; and yet, because of our pre-conceived ideas, we had been nervous about going. We share those kinds of experiences with our people to inspire them and help them understand how the equipment they make is impacting lives in the different countries.

We don't utilize the latest and greatest technology in our products, but we provide a radio that's easy to use. And that's just what a lot of countries need. We went into Afghanistan when they first started building up the military there, and 80 percent of the recruits coming into the military couldn't read or write their own language. So the general came to me and said, "Art, I need a radio that's easy to operate. I have to teach people how to read and write and how to use a radio, and I have about a three-month period to do that before I deploy them." So we listened to what he needed, and we told him we'd be back in about a year. A year later I flew into Kabul and delivered the new radios to the general in his office. I said, "We developed this radio just for you." He said, "Art, thank you very much. No one has ever developed a product just for me. They're always trying to sell me something that they're already selling to other people." When we share stories like these with our people, we find that they're inspired and led to do things that our competitors don't do, and they make the world a better place by doing so.

Champion Your Organization's Purpose

Twelve years ago, we established the Datron Charitable Fund, and since then we've put 10 percent of all profits into the fund. Because of our faith, Lori and I believe we should give 10 percent, or a tithe. We didn't think it was right to give all of that money to our home church; we've let the employees decide where that money goes. Employees can submit grants to our charitable committee, and the committee reviews and approves each grant. In the twelve years since we started the fund, we've given away a little over $15 million in grants to organizations around the world.

That's how we get our employees to *live* our purpose and values. They love being able to positively impact charitable organizations that have helped them or their families by giving back to them through our charitable fund. They tell us who they want to help out and why, and we do everything we can to make that donation happen. This really inspires our employees. We talk to them about what we do through the charitable fund and why we do it. We let people see our hearts. That's something that a lot of leaders don't do.

By telling the stories about our organization and how we're making a positive difference in people's lives, both with our products and through our charitable work, we champion our purpose. When our people latch onto that purpose, it's unbelievable what they'll do.

When Katrina hit in 2005, a couple of our people wanted to donate some radios to help with the recovery during the first couple of days. They tried to get in touch with the Louisiana National Guard; but when they couldn't reach them, they reached out to the California National Guard for help. A representative of that group told them, "Yes, we're going to deploy some equipment there in two days, and we'd love to have some military radios." Our employees got a list of what they needed, and they came to me and asked, "What do you want us to do?" I was smart enough to just get out of the way and let them do it. I said, "You guys go make it happen." The team had the equipment made, packed, inspected, and ready to go, all within twenty-four hours.

After we got the equipment ready, a colonel with the California National Guard came to me and said, "Art, we don't have a way to get the equipment up to Sacramento." He said, "We're trying to get a Black Hawk helicopter to fly in to one of the airports down here to pick it up." The problem, of course, was that the red tape of the United States government wouldn't allow that to happen. I was sitting in the parking lot at Palomar Airport with the colonel, and he was on the phone trying to put it together. I said, "Colonel, they're not going to let you make it happen. Let me talk to some companies here and see what I can do." It was about six o'clock in the evening, and I started calling some of our local air charter companies. When I reached someone in one of the companies, I explained, "We need to get this equipment up to Sacramento around midnight tonight." The company representative said, "Let me call some pilots." Within the hour they had a King Air for us. I went back to the colonel and said, "Here's what's going to happen. We're going to load all the equipment onto a King Air and we're going to fly it up to Sacramento. Tell me what airport it needs to go to. We'll make sure this equipment gets on that C-130 to Louisiana." The colonel said, "But we don't have the money to pay for that." I said, "You don't have to pay for it. We'll make it happen." He was dumbfounded; when he called his general, he said, "I can't believe what they're doing. Here, you talk to Art, the CEO, and he'll explain what's going on." So we loaded the equipment onto the King Air, flew to Sacramento that night, and met the general on the tarmac about one o'clock in the morning. We loaded all of the equipment into his suburban, and it made it on to the C-130 the next morning.

After the California National Guard returned from assisting with Katrina the colonel wanted the Datron employees to see the communications trailer that our equipment was installed in. He also wanted to share some of their experiences with the equipment (all good by the way). It was late summer, early fall in Vista when the weather is perfect for a barbecue in the parking lot. We scheduled the event and the colonel and his staff arranged for the vehicles to be on site in the Datron parking lot. As you can imagine, having a military green Humvee with a large trailer attached with some fairly large antenna's created quite the buzz with our neighbors in the industrial park. That day our employees heard about how their hearts and equipment positively impacted the lives of others. Below is a photo of the colonel and one of his staff with me in the parking lot.

That is what pulls people in a company together—when they team up to make something like that happen, and they do it just to help other people. When you give people a purpose, you can't stop them. They become the champions of your purpose. I'm so fortunate, because as the CEO I get invited to events because of what my employees have done for organizations. It's not me; they've done it all. I get to share the stories and sometimes receive awards, and I always say, "You need to recognize my employees, because it just amazes me what these people have done with their hearts."

If more leaders would lead with their hearts, we could impact the lives of a lot more people.

Behaviors and Language of Servant Leaders

We have identified nine behaviors that we believe are prevalent in servant leaders:

1. Serve first—putting others above yourself in all that you do.

2. Build trust—trusting yourself and extending trust to others.

3. Live your values—letting your words, actions and behaviors reflect your core values.

4. Listen to understand—caring enough to listen to others first; a form of love.

5. Think about your thinking—observing and questioning how and why we think the way we do, to really understand who we are.

6. Add value to others—investing your time in other people's lives; the positive difference you make in them.

7. Demonstrate courage—having tough conversations to help others face challenges and deal with the unfolding of life events.

8. Increase your influence—using your behaviors to influ-

ence others by role modeling, coaching, mentoring, and counseling.

9. Live your transformation—having the discipline and courage to stay the course; serving others above yourself, especially during tough times.

How do I apply these behaviors in my own life, remembering to live them day in and day out? Here's my elevator speech about how these nine behaviors relate to my life, within the context of my daily routine:

1. Serve first. The first thing I do in the morning is make coffee for my wife Lori. I serve first.

2. Build trust. When I drive to work each morning, I pass the bus stop for the school. It reminds me of the work we're doing with the school districts. Based on our work with some of our clients in the education system, we understand that trust is an issue.

3. Live your values. On my route to work, I have to get onto the freeway. In order to get on the freeway, I have to live my values by honoring and respecting people who are already on the freeway. I also have to honor and respect the traffic laws.

4. Listen to understand. After I get on the freeway, I usually get on my cell phone and start talking to people. As a servant leader, I need to listen to understand, so I make a habit of listening more than I talk.

5. Think about your thinking. After I finish my calls, I usually have time on the rest of my drive to work to think about my thinking.

6. Bring value. As I walk through the front door of our facility every day, my most important goal is to add value to someone. I make it personal by putting in a person's name. "What person do I need to inspire and equip today?"

7. Demonstrate courage. I go upstairs to my office, and my assistant Lisa goes over my calendar with me. I often say, "Wow! It's going to take a lot of courage today to get all of this done!" Or there may be one or two conversations I need to have that day to help realign the thinking of some of our people so they will better understand what we do and why we do it. As their servant leader, I have to have the courage to do that in a way that will help them be the best they can be.

8. Increase your influence. I may remember someone I want to help by influencing his or her thinking. I may be able to increase my influence by mentoring that person.

9. Live your transformation. It's easy for all of us to give positive feedback to people we like, people we work with really well, and people who are on board with what we're doing. The challenge is what we do with people who aren't on board, aren't happy in life, very rarely smile, and don't have anything good to say. Our tendency as human beings is to stay away from those people. As I think of such an individual, I may ask, "How am I going to add value today to that person I'm having a tough time with?" As leaders, we need to treat everyone equally. Our transformation is lived through our behaviors.

As servant leaders, our full impact comes with living what we teach. We have to boldly embrace these nine behaviors, as they represent the heart and soul of servant leadership. In fact, everything we do, including the language we use, reveals our level of commitment.

When my kids were young, I was fully dedicated to my career. I had made it a higher priority than my own family and even my health. On weekends (well, Sundays, which was all the weekend I thought I could spare), all I wanted to do was spend time recovering mentally and physically from my hard work all week.

My kids, Jennifer and Chris, had other ideas. They would often come to me and ask if we could do things together as a family that day. My standard answer was, "We'll see." After getting this response on a fairly regular basis, I overheard Jennifer, the older of the two, tell Chris one day that "we'll see" meant "no." Based on my past behavior, my kids were smart enough to translate what I thought was a non-committal answer into what it really meant—"no."

Recently I spent some time on the phone with a very special leader I had met just some months before. I'm a member of a select group of leaders who have invested both time and money into learning from some of the best leaders in the world through a monthly conference call. We also spend time one-on-one sharing best leadership practices. On the phone with my new friend, we talked about leadership in our respective companies and discussed our leadership teams. Well into the conversation, my leadership partner asked if she could provide some feedback on what she had observed. "Yes, please do," I replied.

Her first observation was positive reinforcement. She had not heard the word "but" during my entire description of the leadership within our company. She explained how the senior leadership team of her company had thrown their energy into changing the mindset of their leaders. One of their key focus areas was changing the language their leaders used. The first example she shared was their practice of asking others permission to coach them. They use wording that goes something like this: "I sense an opportunity to mentor you; is it okay if I share with you today"? If the answer is yes, they share their observation or feedback. If the answer is no, They say, "Great! Have a wonderful day. I'll talk to you later." I realized she had just done that in our conversation when she asked my permission for her to give feedback.

Her second observation was not as positive. Basically, she "busted" me on using the word "try" when describing our company's leadership. I think most of my talking points had started off with, "We try to...." She very politely helped me understand how the use of this word really provides a basis for *not* doing something, rather than being a commitment *to do* something.

This was not my first exposure to the connotation of the word "try." Early in my career I had been mentored about the same word. It was around the time that Nike had come out with their slogan, "Just Do It." My mentor explained that you either do something or not; there is no in between. When you say you'll try, you are not fully committed to the action. You have a safe out to fall back on—"Well, I tried."

The *Merriam-Webster Dictionary* defines the word "try" as:

> To make an effort to do something; to attempt to accomplish or complete something; to do or use (something) in order to see if it works or will be successful; to do or use (something) in order to find out if you like it.[2]

There are several phrases that stand out to me in this definition: "attempt to accomplish," "see if it works," and "find out if you like it." When we use the word "try" in our conversations, the people we are communicating with could receive our words within any one of these contexts. More likely, though, people will define "try" based on their previous experiences, either with us or with other leaders.

We have shared how we implemented servant leadership in our companies and created the Servant Leadership Institute to help others do the same. Let's look at how others might receive my comments on servant leadership if I were to use these concepts of the word "try":

> "We are going to make an effort to implement servant leadership at our company;" or "We are going to use servant leadership to see if it works or will be successful," or "We are going to implement servant leadership to see if we like it."

---

2 Merriam Webster Dictionary, http://www.merriam-webster.com/dictionary/try (accessed January 8, 2016).

Compare these statements to the following commitment:

> "We will be a servant-led organization. I believe that servant leadership is the only way to lead and serve others, and we will be known as a servant-led company."

Early on in our implementation at Datron, our leaders thought that servant leadership was just the latest "fad," and that it would be replaced with something else within twelve months. Their reaction was not directed to me as an individual, nor was it directed to the concept of servant leadership. It was based on the fact that the leadership of the company over the previous ten years had spent a lot of money and effort "trying" different leadership styles to "see if they liked it" or "to see if it worked." They never committed themselves to operating their business in any particular way. Does that sound familiar?

As I was listening to my new friend politely bust my leadership language, I realized that this little blip in my language—and hence in my thinking and that of my team—was hindering our company's servant-led culture.

I took over eight pages of notes during our hour-long phone conversation. I am still "thinking about my own thinking"—about the words I use as the CEO, about their impact on others, and about the mindset I have on the language of a servant leader.

Where do you stand as a leader? Are you fully committed to a leadership style? How do those you influence translate the words you say as a leader? Do you use words like "we'll see" or "we're going to try…"?

In the end, we leaders need to show our commitment to those we influence. Our message must be clear. When we're in a senior leadership position, our words send messages to others that reveal the level of our commitment to serve them. I am thankful for this leader's servant heart. Those I serve will feel her leadership influence through the change in my behavior.

PERSONAL	**TEAM**
1. Do you have a purpose?	1. Does your team have a purpose?
2. Do you know your values?	2. Does your team have values?
3. How do you communicate your purpose and values?	3. How does your team communicate your purpose and values?
4. Do you champion your purpose?	4. Who champions your team's purpose?
5. How do you live your purpose?	5. How does your team live their purpose?
6. Assess yourself on the nine behaviors (1–10)	6. Assess your team on the nine behaviors (1–10)

————————	SERVE FIRST	————————
————————	BUILD TRUST	————————
————————	LIVE YOUR VALUES	————————
————————	LISTEN TO UNDERSTAND	————————
————————	THINK ABOUT YOUR THINKING	————————
————————	ADD VALUE TO OTHERS	————————
————————	DEMONSTRATE COURAGE	————————
————————	INCREASE YOUR INFLUENCE	————————
————————	LIVE YOUR TRANSFORMATION	————————

7. What do you need to improve?   7. What does your team need to improve?

_____

_____

_____

_____

_____

_____

_____

Chapter One Table Talk Questions

2

Educate to Own

"Educating the mind without educating
the heart is no education at all."
—Aristotle

Servant leaders understand that our learning will never end.
Neither does our role as educators. If we are to be successful
in our goal of inspiring and equipping those we influence to
be the best they can be, education must be a constant, ongoing
process. And education in and of itself is not enough. In order
to have a deep impact and see real transformation, to see our
people become committed and engaged as never before in the
process of serving others, we must educate to the point of ownership (or, as Aristotle says in the quote above, we must educate
the heart).

Spreading the Word

How many notebooks can you count in your bookshelf
from the conferences and seminars you've attended over your
career? More than five? More than twenty? Now, how many of
those notebooks did you refer to, or even open again, after you
returned from the conference? If your answer was even one, I
would guess that you are in a vast minority. My observation is
that most of us put the book on the shelf with the best intentions; but in the busyness of life, the contents never see the
light of day again.

We love to attend and send our people to conferences, seminars, and training sessions, and the material is usually top notch. Most conferences feature outstanding speakers who offer up just the information and motivation we need to help us overcome challenges and move to another level in our thinking. Some conferences even have the potential to be life-transforming events, given half a chance. But if we just put the notebook in the bookshelf and let the impact get cold, not much transformation will occur. We've been educated, but we don't yet have ownership of what we've learned.

The challenge, then, is how do we overcome that disconnect? What will make us be more intentional about spreading the word—applying what we've learned and implementing it back in the workplace, rather than letting the day-to-day grind bury the answers in the bookcase? What's the missing link between education and ownership?

Another challenge I've observed in the last couple of years is that conferences are not designed to reach multiple generations at the same time. My generation—in their fifties and sixties—love to make full use of the three-ring binders we're given at registration. We flip through them and diligently follow along with the speakers, and we fill the notes pages with all of the things that catch our attention. But those in my son's generation—the twenty-thirty somethings—usually don't even open their notebooks.

The first time I observed this situation was when my son and I attended a conference together a couple of years ago. Noting his lack of interest in the three-ring binder, I asked him about it over lunch. He had decided in the first ten minutes that the conference was old school and had nothing to offer him. He had not even opened his binder to see if there was anything in there worth learning. This intrigued me, and I put our think-tank team at Servant Leadership Institute to work. If we're going to educate to train the younger generation to the point of ownership, we have to figure out what that means. How do we reach them? What's the best way for the different generations—the fifties and above, the forties, the thirties, and the twenties—to learn? The reality is that they've all basically grown up in societies that are vastly different from each other, and we have to figure out how to get into their worlds to educate them.

Mark Babbitt, CEO and founder of Youtern, is described in his biography as "a serial mentor who has been quoted in the *Wall Street Journal, Mashable, Forbes,* and Under30CEO. com regarding job search, career development, internships, and higher education's role in preparing emerging talent for the workforce." In his online article, "25 Jobs in a 50-Year Career: Is Gen Y Ready?" he offers these talking points:

- By 2020, 40 to 50 percent of all income-producing work will be short-term contracts, freelance work and so-called "Super Temps."
- The length of a career is already averaging forty-eight years; by 2020 it will be fifty-plus years.
- The average time in service at any one company for millennials is currently 2.6 years.

Babbitt goes on to say, "2.6 years per job, over 50+ years, plus a couple temp assignments and contracts… and Gen Y is looking at twenty to twenty-five different jobs over the course of their careers."[3] In that case, an organization would have roughly two years to impact the mindset of employees in that generation. How do you inspire, equip, and transform a mind in two years?

And here's something that makes educating that generation to be servant leaders even more challenging: *Time Magazine*'s cover story on May 20, 2013, was entitled, "Millennials: The Me Me Me Generation."[4] Author Joel Stein claims mil-

3   Mark Babbitt, "25 Jobs in a 50 Year Career: Is Gen Y Ready?" Youtern, http://www.youtern.com/thesavvyintern/index.php/2013/10/09/25-jobs-in-the-next-50-years-is-gen-y-really-ready (accessed October 20, 2015).
4   Joel Stein, "Millennials: The Me Me Me Generation," *Time*, May 2013, http://time.com/247/millennials-the-me-me-me-generation (accessed October 19, 2015).

lennials are known for being narcissistic. Much of this came as a result of their baby-boomer parents' obsession with improving their kids' chances for success by raising their self-esteem. An attitude of entitlement and "the world revolves around me" was a natural outcome of that. But he acknowledges that a lot of it had to do with the technology they grew up with, even suggesting that we of the older generations may have ended up with the same qualities had we had access to the technology of today. "A lot of what counts as typical millennial behavior is how rich kids have always behaved," he said. "The Internet has democratized opportunity for many young people, giving them access and information that once belonged mostly to the wealthy." He ends the article with a more rounded picture of millennials, saying, among other things, that they are earnest and optimistic, they embrace the system, they are pragmatic idealists, and they are less rebellious than previous generations. We need to look no further than millennials like Mark Zuckerberg to see that they are making a huge, positive impact on our world with their fresh ideas and approaches.

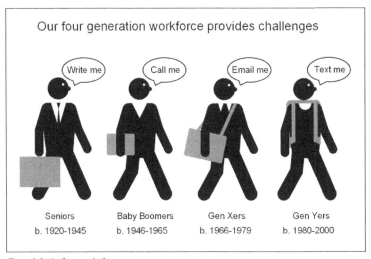

Copyright/reference info:
https://www.evolllution.com/wp-content/uploads/2012/10/challenges-of-the-four-generation-workforce.jpg.

Here's my point in all this: This larger-than-ever class of people in our society is taking the workplace by storm, and they are our new emerging leaders. Just as they have much to offer with their unique societal characteristics, we have to come up with unique techniques to educate and train them if they are to become the servant leaders of tomorrow. We should be training them to show up at organizations and say, "How may I serve you?" rather than "What do you have for me?"

Even though we don't have all the answers yet at SLI, we're working hard to connect the dots between education and ownership, and we're partnering with organizations that focus on various generations to try to figure out how our content can be amended to reach the people they serve. Currently, we are in partnership with the City of Carlsbad in a program called Carlsbad Student Leadership Academy (CSLA)—a program designed to teach student leaders about servant leadership. The program to date has graduated three classes, with a fourth in progress. I compliment the City of Carlsbad for funding this program to develop the young leaders in their community and to help them discover a life of serving.

Add Value to Your Leaders through Education

When we first started implementing servant leadership at Datron, I spent some time sharing tapes and DVDs to get my point across. I found myself frustrated, though, because my team just wasn't getting it. Thankfully, it didn't take me long to discover an interesting truth about the educational process I was using: as long as *I* was driving that process, my management team didn't own it. Finally, I told my team during a management session, "Okay, as the leaders of Datron, *you* develop a list of the characteristics you think servant leaders should have." So they broke off into groups, and after a couple of hours of discussion each group came up with ten characteristics. Then I told them, "Okay, get all the groups together and come up with one composite list." In the end, they came up with a very commanding list of the ten characteristics they believed a servant leader should have: integrity, visionary, humility, listener/communicator, accountability, mentor, honor/respect, compassion/empathy, empowering, lives the values of the company. *They came up with this list; I didn't participate in that discussion at all.* When I look back, I can pinpoint that as the day we moved from educate-to-train to educate-to-own. When the management team started owning the implementation process, that's when things really started to click. (Please note that this list of characteristics of a servant leader represents the way the leaders at Datron see the role. Each organization should take ownership of its own list of the characteristics they believe servant leaders should have.)

As a leader, I'm always asking, "How do I add value to the education of our people?" One of the most important factors, I think, is making sure the leader's voice is in that education. Everyone on the team needs to be speaking with the same terminology and saying the same things about the organization, especially what leadership means to them. At Datron, we have two different definitions of leadership with two different levels of commitment. Our Leadership Council is a team of individuals who want to take on the additional responsibility of making a difference within the company. They actively support the values, mission, and purpose of the company and wholeheartedly embrace and embody the servant leadership culture through their behaviors. Before they are voted into the Leadership Council, new members must complete a rigorous training regimen, including mentoring, classes, conferences, reading, and small group participation. On the next level, the management team is made up of individuals who say, "You know, I like my job as a manager. I enjoy what I'm doing, and I don't want to take on that additional responsibility of working with a team that solves the overall problems of the company." These people are great managers; they just have a different level of commitment.

You can only spread yourself so thin. At some point you have to ask, "Where is the best place to spend my time adding value?" It took me a long time to come to the conclusion that, as the senior leader, the best thing I could do was focus on and add value to a small group of people. I decided that our Leadership Council—the people who want to take on additional responsibility, solve the problems of the company, and be responsible for the overall health of the organization—was where I needed to invest my time.

You also need to add value with the content of your education. It doesn't do your organization much good if your training content is only geared toward a college student in an advanced degree program. If you have multiple PhDs, for example, that's the world you probably think in, and you may have a hard time reaching the hearts of those outside of that educational level.

In considering how to add value to your organization, you must understand the generations as well as the capabilities of your people so you can develop the content for every level. You want to serve them all well by teaching them in a way that will help them own the concepts and move them into their day-to-day processes.

Investing Your Time for the Good of the Organization

Another question I ask is, "How can I best spend my time to help move the training along?" I used to go to every session and talk about values for about five minutes, and then attend the graduation at the last class. That was easy to do; it was a relationship thing, and I loved doing it. Eventually, though, I came to realize that it was better for me to invest my time with those who were struggling with their transformation, rather than with those that were doing well. If I want to live my values of helping people get better, I need to help those who are struggling, and that's where I think I can do the most good for the organization.

Sometimes we don't want to spend time with people who don't get it; we want to stay away from them. One of our servant-leader behaviors, though, is increasing our influence.

What that means for me is spending time with people on the management team that I don't have the best relationship with and increasing my influence with people who don't get it. I'm already influencing those who do, so I can increase my influence even more if I go talk to people that I need to create a more positive relationship with. Most of the time that involves walk-around time. I might go spend some time with them when I see them outside on the patio at break time. Or I may make sure I mention something positive to them when I meet them in the hallway, and not just walk by and ignore them. At one point I realized that showing indifference to people creates a lot of damage, so I've learned to engage and say something positive. Don't get me wrong. I'm not perfect this area. I still have times where I just want to walk away and ignore them; but, I believe I'm getting better.

Investing time in those who are struggling with what you're trying to teach can prove to be a big boost in their transformation. Sometimes they just need an encouraging word, like "Hang in there." Sometimes I need to say, "Hey, listen. I know you're moving forward. I see positive progress. Don't worry about comparing yourself to everyone else on the management team. As long as you're making progress, that's what we're looking for." And sometimes just a "Hi" in the morning is a big plus.

Understanding How to Live Your Education

I stepped down as the CEO of Datron for several years, and I came back to that position early in 2015 with the mindset that I needed to pass on everything I know to my senior team. My role today is not to run the company, although I do have things I run; my role is to bring up future leaders and pass on my knowledge to them.

My senior leadership team at Datron has a deep desire—almost a sense of urgency—to learn as much as they can about the business. The team consists of leaders with an average of about six years with the company. I've been in the business since

1997, and they want to know how I think and how I am able to see the things I see. Datron is a multicultural international business with very interesting challenges. They often ask questions like, "How can you look at something and know where you want to go with that?" or "How do I put your knowledge to work in my mindset?"

We were in a management team meeting a few months ago, and the senior leaders were talking about what they were learning about the business. One of the other managers on the team asked, "How do you feel about Art investing his time to pass on his knowledge to you?" One of my senior leaders spoke up and said, "You know, I've learned more about the business in the last three months than I have in the last three years." I thought, "That's what it's about! We can tell people what to do, and we can put guidelines in place to get them to do what we want them to do. But if they don't understand the business, they're not the leaders we need." We have to get people to live and apply what they've learned.

It's great to have an academic degree, but you have to put that together with experience. Once you combine your knowledge with your experience, add leading with your heart to that equation. You really have the ability to increase your influence with people in a powerful way when they are funneled through your heart.

$$\text{Education (Academics) + Experience} =$$
$$\text{Influence + Heart} = \text{Influence}^2$$

Take any part of that equation away and you lose a huge measure of your influence. When you apply your heart to your education and experience, your influence will be unlimited. Lead with your heart and discover no limits; that's when you can really make a difference in people's lives.

Small Groups

In my early years as CEO of Datron, we would get the entire management team together—about thirty to thirty-five people—for two-day quarterly off-site meetings. On the first day, we would do presentations and share information; on the second day, we would solve problems. In those meetings, I observed that there were certain individuals on the team who never participated. I tried many different things to engage them, like asking them outright for their input, but I was never successful in getting them really involved. I finally came to the conclusion that some people just had a fear of speaking out about the challenges in the company and what was needed to solve those challenges when the CEO was in the room. There were some on the management team who were never going to participate as long as I was in the room, even though I had proven myself through my servant-leader behaviors. They could not change their mindset that said, "I can't tell the CEO the real problems we have."

So in order to help people with their transformation to servant leadership, we decided to follow what we learned through the church—create small groups. We made sure that each group was made up of only peers and did not include anyone on the level above them. We asked them to meet in their groups once a month.

When we first started the small groups, the managers said, "Okay, Art, what do you want us to talk about?" I said, "You set your own agenda. This meeting is for you. It's not for me, so I don't want to set your agenda, and I don't even want a report on what you discuss or on your progress." They said, "So you don't want to tell us how to do it, you don't want to set the agenda, and you don't want a report. Then why are we doing this?" I said, "To give you a forum where you can be yourselves, share information, talk about your challenges, and get help from your peers." I said, "This is about leader transformation. It's about growing you as leaders."

Since that time, all of these groups have met for an hour each month, minimum; some groups meet more than that. After about two years, there was some question about whether we should change the makeup of the groups and move people around. So we started down the path of determining who should meet with whom, noting that some people didn't get along that well together. Interestingly, though, the groups came back and said, "No, we don't want to change. We're really starting to see how we can help each other; we're seeing some progress. We want to stay together." So we stepped back, and they're still meeting today—every month.

What we accomplished with the small groups was to create a safe environment for leaders to talk about their challenges with their peers. In that mode, they are able to take what they've learned and talk about the problems they have in transforming their thinking into that of a servant leader. And because of that safe environment format, we saw transformation really start to take off. Here are a few comments from some of our people about the impact the small groups have had on them:

> As a manager, there is a load on my shoulders to make sure I am always doing the right thing, especially in difficult circumstances. Small group allows me to share and listen to concerns, challenges, and opinions in a way not found in other settings. Using fresh eyes from others gives me a new perspective on these concerns and challenges and helps me set a proper course."
> —Bill Luckow

> Small groups give you the opportunity to let your guard down and be true to your feelings, which helps you embrace them and grow from them. —Joe Parent

> I found the small group particularly helpful when I first joined Datron, as it helped me adapt quickly to the management style and with the management team. The most important aspect of the small group is the fact that discussions stay within the group, and various levels of management (by rank or years of experience) get to share their challenges as equals. —Anonymous

> I work remotely, and the small group makes me feel

included, as if I didn't work from a remote office at all. It gives me an opportunity to interface and build stronger relationships with coworkers I don't have frequent contact with and eliminates the distance between the office locations. —John Biljan

The small groups have been a tremendous help to me, as well, because I no longer stayed frustrated about the lack of progress or the lack of participation in the meetings. It took a while for me to realize that I had been expecting everyone to transform at the same speed. These small groups gave people the ability to transform at their own speed, based on their own mindset, without any pressure from me. I began to realize that my job was figuring out how to take all these people who were transforming at different speeds and still keep them focused together on getting results in the business. I had to change my mindset to become the keeper of the puzzle, so to speak, and focus on putting the right pieces together to get the right results. (Note: We will talk more in Chapter Four about what transformation looks like and how to measure it.)

Another very positive outcome of these small groups is the drastic reduction in onboarding time when a new leader is brought in, whether that person has just started with the company or has been promoted from within to a leadership position. The new leader can pull from the experience and knowledge of his or her more experienced peers in a safe environment and allow relationships to develop, without having the pressure of interfacing with the boss in those meetings.

Several years ago, we were challenged by two different leaders with very different backgrounds. Our vice president of sales was in his sixties and had been with the company about twelve years, while our vice president of marketing was in his early forties and had been with us for about two years. Both of them were very bright individuals, but were obviously from different generations. We didn't see the progress we expected in getting them to come together in a similar mindset until we got them into a safe environment where they could just talk—not worrying about how they came across or trying to impress each other, just getting together to talk. They are both great assets for the company, and we knew they had the potential to do amazing things together. When a leader provides the opportunity for people to get together like that in a safe environment, without any pressure of expectations other than to just create a great relationship, it gives them an opportunity to get to know each other. When they work amicably toward a common mindset, it makes it easier to work together toward the common goal of getting great results, rather than just working together because the boss said they had to.

Creating Team Memories

When we started seeing success early on—soon after we bought the company—we decided to reward the management team with an annual off-site meeting, and we started with Hawaii. Our goal was to reward members of the management team for their hard work for the year. We knew that spouses were a big part of that success, so we invited them to join us. We also wanted to include some leadership training and team-building in the annual events, and we wanted to create some great memories for the team.

That first year we held this off-site meeting, we spent the first morning talking about the business, and in the afternoon we held a golf tournament. It wasn't just for golfers; it was for everyone. We made up some rather goofy rules so people could just have a good time together on the golf course, and everyone could win something. It was a huge success. Everyone had a blast, and some great relationships began forming.

Each year, we've brought in a speaker for a day, usually someone like John Maxwell or Stephen M. R. Covey—speakers who would really make a difference for our leaders. We normally focus on just the management team in the morning, so the managers spend three hours with the speaker we bring in. In the afternoons, we have the spouses join us, and the speakers do something for our team members and their spouses, usually something that will strengthen the couples in their relationships and that they can implement in their family lives. The first year we did that it was a little uncomfortable because people didn't understand what we were doing.

I think it was the third year that we brought in Dr. John Izzo. I had heard him speak before on discovering the five most important things you want to do before you die. He took our leaders and their spouses through a process with breakouts, where couples talked about what they wanted to accomplish together, where they wanted to go, and what they wanted to change in their lives. We had no idea where that was going to lead. But most of the couples, including Lori and I, shed some tears before it was over because we had to talk about what we wanted to be. At the end of this session, John said, "If these five things that you and your spouse agreed on through this process are so important to you that you want to accomplish them before you die, then why aren't you doing them right now? Why are you putting them off?" The room got really silent. It was a pretty intense, life-changing afternoon for most of us.

Fred, who was our vice president of marketing and sales at the time, called me a couple of weeks later and said, "Art, I think this teambuilding stuff is going to backfire on you." I said, "What do you mean, Fred?" He said, "Well, one of the things on my list is to spend more time with my grandkids; so I want to sit down and work with you on my retirement plan." I said, "Okay, Fred, we'll do that." We supported Fred in this request (that's what servant leaders do) and helped him reach one of his personal goals before he retired. When he decided to step down we asked him to serve on our Advisory Board, and he agreed. Fred has now retired twice and is scheduled to retire again in December 2017. He comes back and helps out when we need him. He and his wife Debbie have told Lori and me many times, "You tell us what you need. We will do *anything* for you! *Anything!*" As a leader, when you help others accomplish their goals and work with them on what is important, you will form lifetime friendships that are priceless.

Over the years, we've had several of those events that help our leaders improve their relationships with their spouses and strengthen their families. In addition, we always have a day where we do teambuilding activities to strengthen relationships within our team. A couple of times we hired a company to come in and conduct an activity that involved using electronic devices to find pods that had been placed in some pretty interesting places around the resort. The purpose of the game was to have the teams realize they couldn't get to all the pods by themselves, and they had to start working together (just like departments within an organization). We did one of these on a fifty-five-acre resort, which was a pretty amazing course for the teams to go through. We've also done it at smaller venues, and we did it once on an island, with the teams using Jeeps to search the island as they were playing the game.

The most memorable teambuilding event we've had, in my opinion, is one that cost very little, because we didn't bring anyone in to conduct the activity. In his book, *The Speed of Trust*, Stephen Covey told an interesting story: Doctors at a pediatric hospital in England realized an urgent need to improve the procedures they used to hand over a patient from the operating team to the recovery team in the intensive care unit (ICU). That critical transfer of patient, equipment, and information was very high risk, and mistakes were often made, especially since the operating team had sometimes been working for up to eighteen hours. One day one of their doctors happened to be in the doctors' lounge when a Formula One car race was on TV. As he watched, he realized that the hospital's handover from the operating team to the ICU team was similar to the pit stop in a car race, where the team completes the tasks of changing the tires and fueling the car within a matter of mere seconds. So a delegation of doctors from the hospital went to meet with a Formula One racing team in Italy to learn how a Formula One pit crew operates. What they learned from the racing team about pit stops was used to develop and improve the handoff between the operating room team and the recovery team. The handoff in the hospital improved by 50 percent, which resulted in lives being saved.

We came up with the idea of having our own motor car race, complete with pit stops. We bought two battery-operated kids' cars (I think they cost about $400 apiece), and we shipped them to Hawaii. Somehow we convinced the hotel to let us create our own racing track inside a ballroom by putting tables on their sides. Part of the racing track included an area for pit stops, where the results of working together as a team would be experienced.

Since the cars had been shipped unassembled, the two teams spent the first day putting their cars together. One team had a lot of manufacturing people, and they set up tables and laid out all of the parts and screws. They were very organized— like an assembly line. The other team had fewer hands-on people and more visionaries. They were just going through all the parts, trying to make something happen. It was hilarious to watch. Then, on the second day, we actually had car races— inside the ballroom!

Even though this may have been the most fun event we had ever had, our teams learned a lot. Once the cars got to the pit stop, the teams had to work together to switch the front and back tires, and sometimes they had to take things apart and put them back together again. In preparing them for the race, we told them, "Before the race starts, you can discuss with the team who's going to take what position during the pit stop. Figure out what needs to be done, determine what each team member is good at, and put them to work there. But once you jump over the fence into that pit, you all have to work together, using the same plan and doing your best to get that car out of the pit as fast as you can. That is *not* the time to discuss who's going to do what." That helped us reinforce planning and putting people in their gifts.

We all had a lot of fun racing those cars around the ballroom. When the competition ended, the teams wanted to continue racing. They were having a great time together, creating memories from experiences that will last them a lifetime. As leaders, we need to create experiences where our teams can have fun together, learn about working together, and then spend a lifetime reminiscing about it. At the end of the day, we decided to leave the cars there and give them to some kids on the island, leaving a meaningful impact on the community.

Another year, we stayed on the island of Lanai in Hawaii. It's one of the smallest islands, and they only have one small town and two hotels. The town's library needed painting on the outside, so we decided to paint it. Everyone showed up that day, including the spouses, and we went to work. The town didn't know what hit them, with our people climbing all over their library and painting. They had a blast watching us and kept asking, "What are you doing here? Why are you doing this?" We replied, "We're just doing it to help." Our team enjoyed it so much that we decided the next year to paint the senior center. We finished painting the entire building just before lunch time. The locals had prepared lunch for us and honored us with stories from the oldest person on the island. I remember sitting in the park watching my team enjoy this special time together.

We like to create the kind of events that the team will remember and talk about forever, like the memories a family creates for its kids. An interesting takeaway from this is our leaders are constantly thinking about how they can create new experiences for the new leaders we bring in, who weren't part of our past experiences. They want them to have their own memories and be able to build relationships within the organization through those kinds of activities. When we bring in people from large organizations, most of them have never seen anything like this before, and getting them to let go and have fun and not worry about how they're seen is an interesting transformation for them.

In the summer of 2015, after I had stepped back in as CEO, we decided to have another one of those inexpensive team-building events. This time we chose to mimic the business processes of our radio division. We set up a game that required two teams to build a Lego cargo ship. The process began the night before; bid notices were issued to the teams electronically, notifying them that the bid requirements would be issued the next morning at 7:30 a.m. Responses to the bids were due at noon that day, with one important rule: The bid responses could only be prepared during the breaks, not during the morning sessions. Once the bids were submitted, they were reviewed, and the contract awards were made at 4:00 p.m. that day. The teams had until 9:00 p.m. that evening to build their cargo ships. We incorporated many of our normal processes into the game. Both teams finished before the deadline. With this simple, inexpensive game, we created a new experience for the current team that allowed them to work together in a fun environment to build memories that will last forever.

Servant leadership is not easy. It involves a constant, never-ending process of learning and teaching and implementing. We've been servant leaders in the making for eleven years now, and we have not yet arrived—nor will we ever. Obviously, with the challenges we've presented in this chapter, there is still a lot we have to learn.

How about you? We hope you will join us in impacting our world through servant leadership. And if you do, an important thing to understand is the critical need for constantly continuing your own education, and then turning around and teaching those you influence what you've learned.

PERSONAL

1. Is ongoing education a priority for you?
2. How do you take ownership of the education you receive (applying what you've learned and implementing it in your life)?
3. Do you look for ways to add value to anyone you teach or influence?
4. How do you invest your time for the good of the organization?
5. Do you actively participate in any small group sessions that are available to you?
6. What do you need to improve?

TEAM

1. Is ongoing education a priority for your team?
2. Does your team have a process for helping its members take ownership of the education they receive (applying what they've learned and implementing it in their lives)?
3. How does your team add value to the education of its people?
4. How does your team invest its time for the good of the organization?
5. Does your team provide small group opportunities for your people?
6. What does your team need to improve?

_____

_____

_____

_____

_____

_____

_____

Chapter Two Table Talk Questions

3

Empower Ownership:
Not What You Think

"Leadership, true leadership, is not the bastion of those who
sit at the top. It is the responsibility of anyone
who belongs to the group."

—Simon Sinek, *Leaders Eat Last: Why Some Teams
Pull Together and Others Don't*

When someone refers to me as "Owner" or "Ownership," I
feel like I need a crown, a robe, and a scepter to complete
the picture likely visualized by those around me. To me, and I
imagine to others as well, it sounds like a title of royalty, like
"Your Royal Highness."

Ownership Defined

Most people who are brought up in a corporate background are trained to elevate the owners (stockholders) and put
them on a pedestal. Ownership is a privileged title that denotes
control. Not so in our company. Yes, Lori and I are the legal
owners of Datron, but in our culture we don't want to be known
as ownership. We are a servant-led organization where the traditional ownership title and method of operation do not exist.
We do not publish an organizational chart, but we operate our
company by an inverted organizational chart, where the CEO

is at the bottom. We're all in this together. We look at ourselves as part of a team, not as the owners.

In a traditional organizational chart, which we call the "power model," the CEO is always at the top. In the servant leadership culture, we teach leaders to serve first; but in a traditional organizational structure, there's no one above the CEO to serve, except for a board of directors or shareholders—a very limited group. When Ken Blanchard was mentoring me early on in my transformation, he helped me see that in order to change the mindset to one that says our leaders are here to serve everyone in the organization, we must turn that organizational chart upside down and put the CEO at the bottom. Everyone else in the organization is above the CEO. It is a *major* shift in mindset away from the power model where the CEO is at the top, leading from a position of command and control, to the servant leadership model where the CEO is there to serve all employees and see that they are valued and treated with dignity and respect. And in order for me as CEO to have that mindset, I have to look at things differently.

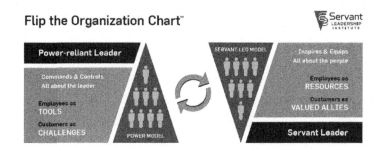

The next level up from me includes my Senior Staff. It helps for me to look at the inverted organizational chart and think, "Okay, here's the group I need to serve first." It also reminds me that if I'm going to go from a high level all the way to the floor level, I have a responsibility to serve everyone in between and let them all know what we're doing and why we're doing it. We consider everyone an owner, and we want everyone to think with an ownership mindset that exudes commitment to the organization's mission and purpose. It's my responsibility as the CEO to communicate that mission and purpose in a way that inspires and motivates the employees, showing them how their jobs have meaning and can impact the world.

Ownership, then, in a servant-led organization is not the people who have the financial ownership of the company. Everyone has a stake in the organization—a stake in accomplishing the mission and purpose by performing their daily activities in a way that will well serve the customers, their fellow employees, and the world around them.

Leadership Team Ownership

In 2005, I made an announcement to the company: "We're going to be a servant-led organization." Naively, I just expected my team to immediately jump on board and follow me. I held many management meetings to try to get them to buy in. In those meetings, there was a lot of discussion about why I was doing this. For a long time I avoided talking about my faith because I was concerned about how that might be perceived. But I finally said to my management team, "You need to know what drives me and why I'm doing this."

I told them the story about meeting Ken Blanchard personally, after reading his books for many years, when he came to my church in 2003. That was the beginning of a relationship with Ken that has blossomed into some amazing times together. The night he came and spoke at my church, he challenged us and said, "If you're a follower of Jesus, it's a mandate that you lead like Jesus." He said, "If you really believe what you say you believe, you don't have any other options than to be a servant leader." That night, he really challenged me in my faith. There were about a thousand people there, and early in his talk he asked people to get into small group circles and talk about leadership. After about ten minutes, he stopped us and asked, "What did you talk about?" People reported from the different circles, and the talks had all been about the normal definitions of leadership. Then he asked, "How many of you talked about Jesus?" Now we were in a church environment; and yet only about ten hands went up out of a thousand people, saying they had talked about Jesus in relation to leadership, and mine wasn't want of them. That was my first clue that my mindset about leadership was so heavily into the corporate, accepted mindset, and that I had to start thinking about my own leadership in a different way.

Please understand that servant leadership is a concept that is highly effective and makes a huge impact on everyone involved and the world at large, whether it is centered around Biblical principles or not. Thousands of companies are transforming away from the power model and to the servant leadership model without any reference to religion. It is a model that works, period. When I speak to others about my reason for changing my mindset to servant leadership, I say, "I'm not here to convert anyone; I'm here to serve and help others. We have people of many different kinds of faith, as well as many non-faith individuals, working in our company—all with a common goal to help other people."

But in my personal experience, exposure to servant leadership through Ken Blanchard was the first half of the equation that really convinced me that I had to change my mindset. The second was a life-changing experience with the Department of Justice—an investigation, actually, of our company regarding the Foreign Corrupt Practices Act (FCPA).

It happened before I bought Datron. Datron was owned by Titan Corporation, a public company headquartered in San Diego. Another company wanted to buy Titan. Shortly after they started their due diligence process, their international attorney decided Datron (me and three other leaders) were probably breaking the law and bribing foreign officials to get business, which breaches the Foreign Corrupt Practices Act. An investigation began internally, which resulted in fifty outside attorneys and accountants showing up on our doorstep. We had to explain every transaction we had done for the previous five-year period, and explain how we did business with our network of companies that represented us in the international marketplace. At that time, Datron had been looking for a new general manager. When this investigation started, those who were being considered for the position mysteriously scattered, and I was suddenly "the man" for the position.

To make a long story short, about three months after the investigation started, we learned two things: 1) They found that we had done nothing wrong, and 2) The investigation had nothing to do with the Foreign Corrupt Practices Act. It turned out that the company that was trying to buy Titan saw a weakness in the corporation's value, and they wanted to exploit that weakness to reduce the acquisition price of the stock by $3 a share. It was a devastating experience that caused us a lot of anxiety.

My personal encounter with Ken Blanchard, followed by that experience with the Department of Justice, really changed my mindset about leadership. Lori and I resolved that if we got an opportunity to buy Datron after the investigation was over, we were going to run it according to servant leadership; we were not going to run it like it had always been run.

I explained all of this to my team in my effort to get them to take ownership of the concept of servant leadership. At that point I was looking for 100 percent buy-in. I didn't realize that I was only going to get buy-in from a certain percentage, that some would buy in on their own time frame, and that still others were never going to buy in.

Transferring Ownership to Your Leaders

You may remember my story in Chapter Two about how I was finally able to cast the ownership of the servant leadership characteristics to my team. At one of our quarterly off-site meetings, when I could see I was getting nowhere in convincing them, I stopped the meeting and threw out the agenda. I asked them to break into three groups and come up with the ten characteristics that they believed a servant leader should have. They did that, and after all of the group reports, I said, "Now I want you to take those three lists and make one list." They came up with one list of the ten characteristics a servant leader should have. It was their definition; it wasn't driven by me. That was the day the ownership of servant leadership was transferred out of my hands and into their hands. It wasn't my saying, "This is how it's going to be."

You have to give your leaders a chance to live their own transformation, and you must create a safe place for them to transform their behaviors. The best way I know to do that is to give them ownership. Let them decide up front what that will look like; it allows them to start their transformation, because they own that definition. The list of ten characteristics that my team came up with that day is somewhat different from our current list of nine behaviors that we believe define servant leadership. But the key point isn't whether the list is right or wrong; it's that once they have ownership of the list, it allows them to start their own transformation.

A Challenge: the CEO's Desire to Control

There will be challenges for any CEO who sets out to transfer ownership of servant leadership into the management team's hands. That transformation is a huge mindset change for CEOs who want to be in control of everything. Being brought up in the public environment of a corporate world, as I was, makes it very difficult to change your mindset to letting someone else have control.

Another challenge is that once you transfer ownership, you can't take it back. You have to stay committed to letting that ownership reside with your team, even if it isn't going the way you think it should go. After your team has latched onto the ownership, your role as a servant leader is to help them be successful in owning the mission and purpose of the company—to give them what they need and inspire them, not to go in and take it back. That is a huge challenge, because in reality the legal owner or CEO is responsible for the end results, and yet you're turning the ownership of the mission and purpose over to your team.

That brings up another challenge: finding out somewhere down the line that you don't have the right people. At that point, you have to make a decision. Do you invest more time helping them with their transformation, or is it better to help them find an organization that will accept them the way they are? And if you have to go with the latter, it could be perceived as your taking back the ownership. Even after all of these years, I still face that challenge, and it usually comes from someone who doesn't even realize that I own the company. And that's just the way Lori and I like it. We don't want people to know that we're the owners. We like for them to see us more as partners. We may get a little bit more criticism because of that, but that's part of leadership.

At the beginning of my transformation, when I got into a stressful situation and things weren't going the way they should, I had to be careful not to let my old behavior as a power leader come out and take over my actions. Sometimes I would jump into that mode so fast that it would leave the wrong message with the leadership team that I wasn't really serious about servant leadership.

Another thing I had to learn was that when you do have to make what I call a "command decision," it's time to stop the discussion and just move forward; just be sure to take the time to explain to your team why you're making that decision.

Remember that I was going through my transformation at the same time as my leaders, and it took me several years to understand how my own behavior impacted the leadership team. Being brought up in the corporate world, I was trained and rewarded for many years for being a controlling leader, and that doesn't go away overnight. In fact, it doesn't go away completely, even after ten years. When times get tough I still have to be careful because I know that side of me will come out. When it does, I have go to the person I was dealing with and say, "I should not have reacted that way." I've learned to challenge myself and ask, "What did I do to generate that response?" It took me a while to get to the point where I started looking inside first. That doesn't happen easily.

Servant leadership has helped me to mature in my personal faith in many ways, but one is in the area of grace. Grace is a major tenet of my faith, because Christ gives me grace anew every morning. He doesn't hold anything over my head from the day before. That's the "vertical" application—grace from Him to me. But grace also has a two-way horizontal application. I have to extend grace to my leaders during their transformation, and they have to extend grace to me. They can't put me up on a pedestal and expect me to be perfect, because I'm going through a continual transformation right along with them. Some people don't understand that. Early on, some of my managers told me, "Art, you have to stay calm and keep your voice level down 100 percent of the time." They wanted me to be a robot. I told them, "If that's what you're expecting from me, I will tell you right now, I will fail you. I'm not perfect, and I will make mistakes." Grace has to be extended in all directions within the organization.

Leaders have to be transparent. They have to stand up and say, "You know what? I messed up. That was my mistake, and I take responsibility for it." That is a very difficult thing for leaders to do. Most corporate leaders want to be perfect, and they don't want to admit when they make a mistake. They want to spin their results in order to buy more time from the board to improve the results. But they need to understand that the people in their organizations usually know when their leaders mess up. If the leaders don't own up to their mistakes, their credibility goes down. They will be more influential by being honest and telling people that they made a mistake.

Patience and Discernment

In working with individuals who are transforming their behavior toward servant leadership, you have to be patient. A key point to understand is that each leader will transform at a different speed. There will be some leaders who will latch onto it, roll into it, and run with it. Others will stand back, waiting for you to earn their trust through the process before they jump in. And some will never buy in; they just don't think it's the right thing to do. That's where patience comes in, because you still have to manage this team, inspire them, and get results, even while you're managing their transformation, or lack of it.

We like to use the analogy of putting together a puzzle when we're teaching this concept. Those people in your organization who latch onto their transformation and can communicate and work together at a much faster rate are like pieces of the puzzle that fit together nicely. But there may be a few pieces of the puzzle out there that haven't yet figured out if they want to jump in. They may even have their own little puzzle going with each other while they're trying to make a decision. But then they may realize, "Hey, we can do more together with the bigger puzzle than we can with our little one. Let's complete this picture."

When we talk to corporations about servant leadership, we tell them, "You're going to have puzzle pieces that will come together and fit into the puzzle really well. And then there may be times when you try to make a puzzle piece fit where you think it goes, and it doesn't fit. You have to take it out and let it transform a little bit more before you plug it back in again. And that takes extreme patience for leaders, because there will be times when you question your own belief about whether you can get the results you need with the process you're going through. That's when you really have to have patience and trust your values. Don't give up. You have to remain true to your values."

Here's where discernment comes in: When you do finally come to the conclusion that you have to let someone go, don't wait too long to do it. In the beginning, we wanted to make sure we had done everything we could to help that person transform, and a couple times we waited too long to make the decision, and we paid for it. We weren't mature enough to understand the breakdown of trust within that leader's organization and the length of time it would take to get it back after we let the leader go. You really have to find that balance: We'll invest up to a certain point; but after that point, if we don't see any progress, it's better for the organization to not put any more effort into helping that person transform.

Another part of discernment is honing your skills at reading people and their body language. You need to understand that when people sit back and cross their arms, when the listening knob in their head is turned off, they're not engaged. Early in my career I spent eight years working in the administration building at Disneyland in accounting. During breaks and at lunchtime we were allowed to walk around the park, and that's where I learned to really read people. I would sit and watch people come down Main Street, and I got to the point where I could tell things like where people were going to stop and take pictures or which families were having a tough day (maybe Dad really didn't want to be there or Mom had had enough with the kids). And that foundation of watching people for eight years is something I really cherish today, because it's helped me read the body language of people and how they're responding. You have to be able to understand nonverbal language that tells how people are reacting—when they turn you off and when they turn you on. The most rewarding experience for me is when I see that light come on in a leader's eyes, when he or she starts to realize, "Hey, I can be a better person because of servant leadership." That's what you should strive for.

And you need to have discernment when dealing with situations in the lives of your leaders. Just a few days ago I had a conversation with one of my senior members who has trouble with migraine headaches. She's a younger leader, and as we were talking over a cup of coffee I encouraged her to not let Datron be one of the factors that cause her migraines. I said, "Datron is not worth that. You have more important things in your life to worry about, like spending time with your family and friends. You need to learn how to turn off that switch on a Saturday, not turn it back on until Monday, and not worry about things here at the office during that time."

She's a very special person who has done a wonderful job since she's been with us, and she has a great heart. But she's going down the same path I went down as a young leader, when I thought my career was everything. I know from personal experience that those who put their careers first will lose some things in the process. In my corporate days, when I was a power leader, I would sit back and take advantage of those people and say, "Hey, you want to work seven days a week? Work seven days a week. That's great!" But in the servant leadership world, we're more concerned about the individual person than we are about the amount of work we're going to get. Now I tell my leaders, "If you can't stay out of here at least one day a week, on a Sunday, and preferably two days a week, then, I may have to force you to. Don't forget, I can turn off your security badge that gets you into the building pretty easily, and I will if I have to."

About halfway into our servant leadership journey, probably around 2007 or 2008, I sat down early one Sunday morning and started sending some emails to my leaders. My thinking was that they would have these emails in their inboxes on Monday morning, and they would be able to see them and react to them first thing. By noon that day—on Sunday—every person I had sent an email to had responded to me. That's when I started to realize that by my sending an email out on Sunday, thinking I was getting a head start on the week, I was setting the expectation that people should respond to the email as quickly as they could. I had to have discernment to be able to think, "This isn't right. I am actually promoting this behavior because I'm sending emails out on a Sunday morning." Today, I'll only do that with people who are on the edge and may be putting too much time in. I'll send them an email on a Saturday afternoon; and if they answer during the weekend, the first thing I do on Monday morning is sit down with them and say, "You failed the test. That was a test to see if you'd respond to emails I send you on a weekend." I do the same thing when they take vacation time. I tell them, "Don't take your computer. If we need you, we'll call you." Then sometimes I test them with an email.

Getting Out of the Way

There are times when the best thing a leader can do is to be quiet and let others take care of things. And there are times when the best thing you can do to help people transform is to stop teaching them and just encourage them, giving them space to work on their own transformations. That's a tricky one because everyone is different. Some people want to have your time and effort on a weekly basis to help them transform. Others will say, "You know what? I get it. Let me work on this; and if I run into a stumbling block, I'll come for your help."

A lot of leaders don't know when to get out of the way and let the people who know how to do the work do the work. That's part of the inspiring and equipping of servant leadership. In the manufacturing arena, where I've spent most of my career, people who build the product know how to build it better than the executives who sit in their offices all day. But I've watched companies try to solve manufacturing problems by getting leaders together in a conference room, bringing in lunch and drinks, and talking about how a product should be made; they never talk to the people who actually do the work every day for a living. They never even ask their opinions. And the same thing happens in the office. Most of the time people who do a particular task know how to do it better than the leaders do, so we need to let them take care of the challenges. We need to bring them into the problem-solving and get out of the way.

We deal with some leaders who don't understand that the best thing they can do with their team is to let them go take care of business, rather than requiring that they check in with them all the time. Some may say they want to do this, but then they think they still have to have indirect control. They may tell their people, "I'm going to let you go to this meeting and make decisions, but you need to keep me informed about the decisions you're making. Send me an email after you get out of the meeting and let me know what decisions were made." What that leader is actually saying is, "You can go to the meeting and make decisions, but then check with me to see if those decisions are right." People soon start to understand that those leaders aren't backing them on decisions, so they go to meetings and say, "Why are we sitting here wasting our time; the leader who isn't here is going to make the decisions anyway?"

One or two of my leaders tell their staff to copy them on all their emails. When I ask them why, they say, "I want to stay up to speed on things." I tell them, "You don't want to stay up to speed on things. You want to make sure things get decided the way you want them decided, so you can stay in control." I look at it this way: If I expect you to trust me, then you should expect that I would trust you. So if I say, "Trust me. I know what I'm doing. I'm going to make the decision on this," then I should be able to extend the same trust back to you and say, "I'm going to teach you everything I know about this business, and I'm going to get you to the point where you can make those decisions. And then you won't have to come back and check with me anymore."

One mistake I've made, though, is letting a leader loose too soon. When you bring in new leaders, it's better to keep them close to you up front, and then let them fly after they've proven that they can make the decisions and take the responsibility. If you bring them in and trust them right up front to make decisions, and then find out six months later that they're not making the right decisions, it's really hard to pull them back in. It's easier to invest more time up front in helping them understand the business and understand why you made certain decisions in the past, including why you have certain policies and procedures in place. When you invest in them to help them make decisions for the first, say, three to six months, they can feel good about themselves and not second-guess their decisions. It's always better to loosen up than to tighten up.

When Leaders Don't Grasp the Empowerment Being Offered

There are some who will never take on the responsibility of their own empowerment. I was asked recently in an interview, "What's the difference between leadership and management?" Leadership is geared toward the purpose of the organization. Leaders take ownership of the vision for the future. They will take on the responsibility of working with other leaders to fix the problems of the organization, even if they're outside of their department.

Managers are those who say, "Tell me what I'm supposed to do, and I'll go take care of it. I'm happy doing that." You have to understand that not everyone is going to be a leader, and that a lot of people are very comfortable just doing their job as a manager. Some people want to stay in that management box. It doesn't matter how hard you try or how many hours you invest in them, that's where they're the happiest. You can try and give them empowerment outside of their job description, and they won't latch onto it. And that's okay. They're simply not interested; it's not what they want to do.

Most of these managers will latch on to the servant leadership concept to a certain extent. For example, if we want the managers to invest 20 percent of their time in their employees, they will latch on to that. But when you get them into a room to talk about the vision and purpose of the company and why they do what they do, they will come back and say, "What you're talking about is great. But once you decide that, tell me what you want me to do to support it." They're really task-driven people, and they like for other people to take care of the overall vision and challenges of the organization.

Leaders will spend time explaining the mission and purpose to their people, so they understand the higher purpose of what they do. Managers are not going to talk to their people about making a difference, because that's not their gift. They don't feel comfortable doing that. When you compare the performance of the departments led by a leader vs. one led by a manager, you can see that the first group outperforms the second in the long run. That's just something we have to understand. Both groups get the results they need, but the first group performs at a higher level.

Sometimes managers will tell us, "I'm not being empowered." But often when we give them that empowerment, they'll come back and say, "I don't want to make this decision." What we've discovered is, they don't really want to be empowered, because they don't want to take the responsibility we've given them; they want to pass it on to someone else, or in some cases pass it back to you.

Listen to Understand

One of the most important behaviors of a servant leader is listening to understand—not just listening to what's being said, but understanding what's being said. People feel empowered when you listen to understand. When we first bought Datron, we talked to our leaders about the importance of listening; but I'm not sure we really understood back then that listening was about understanding. We made the point that we need to listen more as leaders, but we didn't teach our leaders what to do with what they heard.

It's really just been in the last year that I've been looking at empathy as a component of listening. Merriam Webster defines empathy as: the feeling that you understand and share another person's experiences and emotions: the ability to share someone else's feelings.[5] According to that definition, you have to hear what people are saying about their feelings so you can understand those feelings; but you also have to be able to share those feelings to be truly empathetic. So it takes much more than just listening to people tell me about their problems and saying,

---

5   Merriam Webster, http://www.merriam-webster.com/dictionary/empathy (accessed 11/2/15).

"Okay, here's what I think you should do about it," and then going on to the next thing. You really need to feel what that person is going through to understand. Men, especially, seem to struggle in this area. We want to take care of a problem, so when it's taken care of we can check it off the list and go on to the next problem. Empathy doesn't work that way. Listening to understand is all about empathy—really feeling what people are telling us. Once we feel what they are telling us, then we are better able to help them. How can you help someone if you don't feel what they're feeling?

Listening —➤ Hearing—➤ Understanding—➤ Feeling —➤ Helping

Be careful to watch out for your non-verbal body language when you're listening to someone. When I don't understand what people are saying, I have a frown on my face, and a frown can be taken the wrong way. I certainly don't mean anything negative by it; it's just a sign that I'm focused on trying to understand. But most people wouldn't understand that. The nonverbal signs you give out while listening are just as important as the verbal.

Remember, the trait that sets servant leaders apart is that they lead from the heart. Ownership, and all it embraces, is a heart issue. When you empower ownership in your leaders, you grant them the power to take your mission and purpose to worlds yet discovered.

PERSONAL

1. How do you define "ownership"?
2. How well do you operate with an "ownership" mindset?
3. What characteristics do you think a servant leader should have?
4. How well do you do at extending grace?
5. Are you a leader or a manager? What characteristics set you apart as one or the other?
6. How well do you listen to understand?
7. What do you need to improve?

TEAM

1. How does your team define "ownership"?
2. How well does your team operate with an "ownership" mindset?
3. What characteristics does your team think a servant leader should have?
4. Is grace a theme practiced by your team?
5. Is your team made up of more leaders or more managers? What characteristics set them apart?
6. How well do your team members listen to understand?
7. What does your team need to improve?
8. Can you and your team show empathy to others?

_____

_____

_____

_____

_____

_____

_____

Chapter Three Table Top Questions

4

Measure Transformation and Results

"Creating happy employees alone is a success strategy for any organization. But when servant leaders also mentor, teach, and transform them—magic happens."
—Tom Zender, Professional CEO, Mentor, and Author

People often ask me, "Isn't servant leadership soft?" My response is that servant leadership is the most difficult thing I've ever had to do as a leader, because while you're asking people to change their behaviors, you still have to get results. You may remember our mission and purpose statement at Datron World Communications: "We want to be a profitable, self-sustaining communications company that positively impacts the lives of others, today and in the future." Obviously, we can't be profitable and self-sustaining without results. And unless we are profitable and self-sustaining, we can't accomplish the rest of our mission and purpose—to positively impact the lives of others, today and in the future. It's a package deal. You can't put results on hold while you're helping people make the transformation to servant leadership; you have to simultaneously get results while you're going through the process. In our mindset, results are meaningless without the servant leadership culture, but impacting lives is impossible without results. It's easier to go out and get results if you don't care about how you get them. But because we care about *how* we get them more than we care about the results themselves, the journey is much more difficult—but so worth the effort!

Creating a Safe Environment for Failure

So how does a servant-led organization differ from a traditional power-model organization in the pursuit of results? One of the main differences is that servant leaders create a safe environment for failure. I often use a quote by John Wooden: "Failure is not fatal, but failure to change might be." As servant leaders, we realize that nobody's perfect and that we all fail; it's part of being a leader. What's important is that when we do fail, we learn from it and change. In a servant-led organization, people are not judged for failing; on the contrary, they are encouraged to face those failures and use them as a learning tool.

No one likes to use the word "failure." People may say, "We didn't get the results we were looking for," or "It didn't turn out the way we wanted it to." But fear of failure creates a culture of indecision, inaction, and a deferment to the leader to make all the decisions. So our job as servant leaders is to create an environment where it's okay to shoot for something that's a stretch ("audacious goals," as we call them), knowing that if you meet them, it will be great and we will all help you celebrate. If you don't, though, it's not the end of the world. We want people to feel safe failing, knowing that their leaders will help them learn in that safe environment. Because fear of failure is often magnified in front of authority, and some people have such a fear of the CEO that it limits their ability to participate in problem-solving, I sometimes have to step out of a meeting or away from a group in order to create that safe environment. (Part of the difference between leaders and managers is that managers fear not being perfect in front of people; leaders know that failure is part of their transformation and learning process.)

Here's another John Wooden quote I often use: "Success is never final; failure is never fatal." Businesses go through many different cycles. It's pretty easy to create an environment that's safe for failure when things are going well. That doesn't take a lot of creativity, because everyone is on the upswing, feeling good about where your organization is and where you're headed. But when times get tough, keeping that safe environment is difficult. Why? Because as leaders, our first reaction is to go back to our old ways—jumping in and controlling everything. And that's when that safe environment goes away.

So what does "creating a safe environment" look like? With my senior team, it's all about relationships and helping them understand that we're not perfect. Part of our transparency as senior leaders is to be able to stand up and say, "I made a mistake. This one's on me."

Outside of the senior staff, I've found that I have to be sensitive to individuals. Different people will react differently to the ownership you give them, and it's up to the leader to figure out what will work for each individual. Some of our people prefer to have private discussions with me, because the public arena is uncomfortable for them. To others, a safe environment means just sending them off with what they need to do, along with the guidelines they need to operate within. They know they can come back and ask, "Is it okay to go outside of those guidelines?" Sometimes the most effective way to impact individuals is through other people, not directly. For example, I sometimes coach an individual's boss on how to deal with that person, because he or she has such a fear of talking directly to the CEO. Other people will react to encouragement more than they will to constructive criticism, and they prefer a pat on the back or a hand-written note of encouragement. And the best thing I can do for some people is to just stay away from them, give them time and space, and not try and push them through the process. It all depends on the individuals and where they are in their transformation. The point is that leaders can't expect people to come up to their level. Leaders need to meet people where they (the people) are. We'll talk more about this later.

I believe our policy of encouraging our leaders to regularly

THE ART OF SERVANT LEADERSHIP II

invest in their people through one-on-one meetings also contributes to that safe environment. At one point I was working with one of our leaders, a director in the Engineering Department who had served in the military. He was often confused about which hat he was supposed to be wearing—the military leader hat or the business leader hat. We got into a discussion one day about investing time with his employees, and he said, "I have an open-door policy. They can come and see me any time." I said, "Show me your calendar, and that will tell me whether you're investing time in your people, or just investing time in opening your door." Servant leaders are proactive in scheduling one-on-ones. It gives people an opportunity to discuss their failures with their leaders and learn from them how to move on. I have one-on-ones with most of the people that report to me every week. Cheryl Bachelder, who was the CEO of Popeye's Louisiana Chicken, invests one entire day a week to doing nothing but one-on-ones with her people. Opening the door is easy. Scheduling time to spend with people is really where you invest in them and help them grow.

Small Groups

Another valuable step we took in generating that safe environment for our leaders was creating the small groups we talked about in Chapter Two. These small group meetings eliminate immediate bosses from the equation and allow the leaders to develop transparent and trusting relationships with their peers through open conversations. In that safe environment they can talk about the real challenges they are facing in the company. There are strict guidelines to protect that environment: no reports come from the groups, and the leaders are not to talk to anyone else, including other leaders, about what was discussed. What is talked about in small groups stays in small groups. Because of that environment, people really open up about their transformational challenges and successes, and their peers are eager to help them. The support that comes from the small groups continues between the monthly meetings; the leaders often call each other and say, "I tried what we talked about, and it didn't quite get the reaction I wanted. What do you think?" Or maybe they'll go have lunch or a cup of coffee and talk about some other strategies. Meaningful mentoring relationship is created through small groups.

We're a multi-national company, headquartered in California, and we have people in time zones all over the world. Some may be eight hours ahead of us, and some may be fourteen hours ahead. Since the small groups encompass the entire team and may include people in Florida, in Washington, or anywhere we do business internationally, the groups bring in those people outside of the home office by phone. Sometimes that means the group meets at 7 a.m. so the international people won't have to get up in the middle of the night. And they don't schedule group meetings at 9 a.m., because that's lunch time for people on the East Coast. Arranging small group meeting schedules to accommodate our remote leaders helps everyone better understand the challenge of serving others around the world.

Geese and Leadership

I like to compare our transformation as a team to a flock of geese flying in formation. Geese fly in a V formation for a reason. The flapping of their wings creates an uplift for the geese behind them, which increases the efficiency of the flock and allows them to fly about 70 percent farther than they would if each bird flew on its own. If a goose falls out of formation, it experiences a drag, or resistance, from the absence of wind provided by the flapping wings of the other geese. Our team can reach its goals much faster by working together within the power of the flock, trusting the others who are going in the same direction to lift them up along the way.

When the leader in front of the flock gets tired, it rotates out and another goose takes its place. The geese behind the leader honk to encourage those ahead to keep up their speed. Leaders who are out in front and pushing forward get tired.

THE ART OF SERVANT LEADERSHIP II

They need to hear words of inspiration and encouragement, and they need to hear the people on their team flapping their wings with them. Words of encouragement and the sharing of difficult tasks help increase the efficiency of a team. If the honking is not honks of encouragement, it's complaining. And complaining never adds value to the flock.

Here's another interesting thing about geese: If one of the flock gets sick or wounded and falls out of formation, two geese fall out to stay with the fallen one until it is well enough to continue or it passes away. In either case, the remaining geese will join another flock until they can catch up with their own. Imagine this scenario in your company: Someone on your team isn't performing well. Maybe this person is dealing with some personal issues, or perhaps is struggling with what he or she is being asked to do. What would happen if two other people on the team took that person aside and helped him or her get through those challenges, and stayed with the team member until the challenges were resolved? What would that look like in today's work place? In most work places, a person who starts falling falls alone because nobody wants to be a part of it.

Transformation is much easier when our team incorporates the lessons of the geese—to stand by each other when things get tough; to stay in formation with those who are going the direction we want to go, depending on teamwork to get us there; and to enjoy the rewarding experience of being a contributing member of a team.[6]

Measuring the Transformation of Leaders

Our leaders at Datron go through ongoing, continuous transformation. When individuals are selected from the management team to serve on the Leadership Council, there are certain qualifications they must meet:

1. Must have a title of manager or above.

---

6 "Lessons of the Geese," In Search of Me Café, published on youtube.com 9/10/10, https://www.youtube.com/watch?v=hazitrxzhPk&feature=em-share_video_user (accessed 11.23.15).

2. Must actively support the values, mission, and purpose of the company.

3. Must have exhibited an ability to make effective decisions, obtain results, and meet business plans.

4. Must actively participate in management discussions and Active Strategy initiatives.

5. Must be in a current mentoring relationship with a member of the Leadership Council who is outside the manager's functional department.

6. Must actively support and participate in a servant leader small group.

7. Must have attended at least two different classes or conferences focused on servant leadership that have been preapproved by the Servant Leadership Steering Committee.

8. Must have completed the required reading material, as defined by the Servant Leadership Steering Committee.

9. Must be voted in by 85 percent of the Leadership Council.

Members of the Leadership Council are required to attend two conferences a year—the Servant Leadership Institute conference and another servant leadership conference that is not connected with Datron or the Servant Leadership Institute. We want them to experience servant leadership from another perspective, so we send them to a conference of their choice where they can meet and network with people outside of our company.

When we first started, our Servant Leadership Council chose one book each year that we required everyone on the Leadership Council to read during the year, and we talked about the concepts of that book throughout the year. We also encouraged the members to find a book on their own that spoke directly to them. We wanted them to be continually learning. But in today's fast paced, changing world, we now require our leaders to read one book per quarter. In 2016 we read the book *Multipliers: How the Best Leaders Make Everyone Smarter* by Liz

Wiseman. In following quarter, we read *Intentional Living* by John Maxwell.

To create a starting point for our servant leadership culture, we as leaders decided to conduct a 360 survey on our servant leader characteristics (see sample survey form on following page) so our leaders could see where they needed to improve. Then we asked, "How are we going to measure transformation going forward?" We put a couple of things in place that would help us determine how our leaders were progressing.

First, we started surveying the leaders each month to see how much time they spend with the people in their organization in a one-on-one mentoring role. Our goal is for them to invest 20 percent of their time with their direct reports. It's not a scientific process; it's a simple online survey that asks them to estimate the percentage of their time that was spent that month with their direct reports. It took a while for our leaders to get comfortable with these monthly surveys. We assured them that we were not going to use them to demand a higher level of performance or create performance improvement plans. They are simply a tool to help us understand how we are doing as a leadership team on the goal of spending 20 percent of our time investing in our people. We track the surveys each month, and then we talk about the results in our monthly management meetings.

I believe the second measuring tool we put in place has had the biggest impact. We require that our leaders write two short paragraphs each month on two different areas of their transformation. In the first paragraph, they answer the question, "What did I do this month that was a positive experience in my transformation in servant leadership?" In other words, we want them to tell a story about a time during the month when they helped someone. The second paragraph should describe a situation in the last thirty days in which they struggled to be a servant leader. So each month they tell about something they did well and an area where they didn't do so well. Again,

Servant Leadership Survey Form

As a follow up to our discussions on May 18, 2007, please take a few moments to answer the following questions about the Leadership Council member named below. Your open and honest response will help us better understand whether we reflect the ten servant leadership qualities as defined by Datron.

Person You Are Evaluating:

I believe that the Leadership Council member named above reflects the following characteristics of a servant leader.

	Strongly Disagree	Disagree	Agree	Strongly Agree
Integrity				
Visionary				
Humility				
Listener/Communicator				
Accountability				
Mentor				
Honor/Respect				
Compassion/Empathy				
Empowering				
Lives the Values of the Company				

Completed By:

we created a system where they can go online and write those reports. The entire management team has access to the reports, so anyone on the team can look at any of them at any time. Interestingly, though, we discovered that most people don't go in and read the reports; so we started asking one or two leaders to share in the monthly management meetings what they wrote. We normally have one or two leaders who are happy to talk about their reports.

This tool has created a real transparency in the leadership team, because our leaders have had to talk about not only their successes, but also where they struggle. It requires them to take a hard look at those two areas of their transformation every month; and knowing their stories will be shared—online or in the meetings, or both—helps them be more open. The stories that are shared have a huge impact on the other leaders. They can relate to the stories, and they help them realize there are others in the organization who are struggling with servant leadership just like they are. And sometimes after leaders have shared their stories in the management meetings, others will say something like, "You know, this is what I did when I was at that point," or "This might help you." That really helps perpetuate the safe environment for two reasons: 1) we ask them in advance if they want to share their stories, so they are not shared without permission, and 2) other leaders voluntarily offer up advice after the stories are shared. We usually have the stories at the beginning of the meeting, which creates an atmosphere of openness and transparency for the rest of the meeting in the discussion of financial results and where we are with the initiatives we had set.

In the beginning some people wouldn't do the reports, so we had to help them understand that they were a requirement. We would tell them, "You have to do this, but it's going to be okay. No one is going to take you to task for what you write." We reached 100 percent participation, but it took us a while to get there. Very rarely do we have someone say, "I don't have a success story to share this month," and that creates its own positive reinforcement. It forces them to reflect on what they did and helps them realize, "Hey, I did do something positive this month; I've made some progress!" It helps the management team to see that reflection, hear the stories that are shared, see the transformation we're looking for, and be able to talk about both the positives and the challenges.

Managing the Different Speeds of Your Team's Transformation

About two years into our implementation of servant leadership, I was surprised to realize that all of my leaders were not transforming at the same speed. I had naively anticipated that we would all grow together, both as individuals and as a team. What I discovered was that some people grasped the concepts and grew much faster because they were ready for it. They already had the capacity for servant leadership inside of them, and they were just letting it out; so the transformation of their thinking and behavior happened at a faster rate. Then there were others at the opposite end of the spectrum who were still wondering if this was the latest "flavor-of-the-month" management technique. They were either waiting to see if servant leadership was going to hang around before they would invest time in it, or they simply didn't believe in the concept. Some really believed the power model was the best way to get results, and they didn't trust the service model. As a result, their transformation was very slow.

So after two years I had some on the management team who were moving fast, and we were forming a tight, cohesive group. They understood the concepts and knew the language; they were moving forward and making changes, and they understood how to interpret and help their people. Those who weren't able to transform their behaviors as quickly started feeling left behind and wondering how to become part of the other group. It wasn't until a couple of years later that I started to understand how the human brain works, and how the experiences people had before they joined Datron impacted their ability to change. That's when I really started to understand that those who were not grasping the concept and not transforming as fast as the others weren't bad people. Because of their past experiences, they just had a few more hurdles that we needed to help them overcome.

So, as the leader, I was faced with a challenge: having to understand where the different pieces of the management team puzzle fit in their various stages of maturity in servant leadership, while simultaneously helping them perform and be successful together. With the constant, overlying pressure of needing to get results, it was probably the most difficult thing I've ever done as a leader. In order to obtain the results we desired, we still had to perform as a company.

During that year we made a commitment: if we saw progress in the transformation of a person's behavior, we were willing to continue to invest in that individual. Even if we only saw small steps, we would say, "This is great. You're making progress. We'll continue to help you move forward." It was about the same time we started the small groups, and that's really when many of those people began to speed up their transformations. There was still the pressure of having to get results to meet our customers' requirements; but now they could take that discussion into a safe small-group environment without the pressure of having to tell the CEO they didn't meet their goals. Their small group peers could help them with the challenges that kept them from getting the results they needed.

Our commitment to invest in those who were struggling with their transformations didn't come without a price. We hired one person on a director level, who was on the senior staff, reporting directly to me. We invested two years into helping that person transform. There were some personal issues involved, so I brought in someone from outside the company to work with the individual one-on-one. But the transformation never took place; the director continued to get results with the power model rather than the servant leadership model. At the time, my thinking was, *I want to be able to look myself in the mirror and know I've done everything I could to help this person change.* Unfortunately, that thought process led me to hold on longer than I should have.

After two years of investment, we sat down to talk, and I said, "You know, we have to see a change here." The employee looked at me and said, "Art, I don't understand why my leadership approach isn't accepted at Datron. I get results." I replied, "The power model is just not accepted here. We're more concerned with how we get the results than with the results themselves." Then I said, "It's best for us to part ways." "You know," the director said, "I have been working in that leadership model my entire career. I have been rewarded handsomely for meeting quarterly targets. I've been recognized with awards and with bonuses." It was a great point. This person had been recognized and rewarded for years by companies that didn't care about how the results were obtained. I said, "Our role now is to help you find a place that will accept you as you are." And we did that. This person was one of the brightest I've ever seen in the radio business. We spent a little extra money to help this employee find a great job. About eight months later, I received a note from the individual that said, "Art, I realize now what you've done for me. I want to thank you for putting up with me and helping me get through the challenges I faced. I'm a much better person than I was before I joined Datron, so thank you very much."

That individual had managed close to 60 percent of Datron's workforce. After the person left, we discovered that the trust had been badly broken because the power model had been used to get results. It took us about two years to get that trust back. So we paid a very high price, not only in having to hire someone new, but also in having to work to get the trust back in the people who had been used to get results the wrong way. When I look back, I realize I should probably have invested six months into that individual. That was a transformation I went through—I had to learn that I needed to make decisions about individuals sooner, rather than later, when they were not willing to make the transformation.

After we had invested eight years in teaching, training, and learning the servant leadership culture, I thought the servant leadership culture was ingrained deeply enough that I could step down and bring in a new leader. Unfortunately, I learned the hard way that we could drift away from our culture pretty quickly when a new leader (authority figure) came into the picture.

The new leader didn't put the same priority on servant leadership that I did. His behavior indicated that he was not willing to invest in training people, which was contrary to what we had been teaching. But the biggest challenge I had with the new leader was that he created a divisive team. He was a very likeable and smart man—and a very quiet power leader who wielded his influence through kindness. It was an interesting approach.

What he valued and what I valued as investments were in completely opposite realms. Let me give you an example. We have participated in a trade show in Jordan for many years, and we've supported the government of Jordan on multiple programs and projects. The head of defense in Jordan, Prince Faisal, who is the king's brother, wanted us to sponsor a lunch at the next trade show in Jordan.

When his request came to me, I got on the phone with our new vice president of strategic marketing who had been brought in by the new leader. He was not in favor of making the investment because he couldn't see any new business coming out of it. My take on it, from a servant leadership viewpoint, was more about how important the relationship was than whether we would get any additional business from it. We have a great relationship with both the king and the prince there, and we've done a lot of work for them over the years. To me, the sponsorship was a relationship investment, not a sales investment. That's the basic difference between the power model and the service model. The power model says, "If I do something, I want something in return." But the servant leader says, "We're here to help you. We're willing to give you what you need. You can reward us if you feel like we served you appropriately." It's an investment, and most of the time we'll see something out of it because people see that we conduct business differently.

One of the most important things I've learned about managing the different speeds of my leadership team's transformation came from studying what Jesus did, and that's meeting people where they are. I've learned that it isn't about expecting people to meet me where I am. I have to understand where they are and ask myself, "How do I add value to them where they are today?"

When I talk about living your transformation, I always mention that it's easy to live your transformation with people you like and those who are performing well and are on board with servant leadership. It's really tough to live your transformation with someone who isn't on board with you, who is not adding value to people, and who comes to work grouchy every day. We really don't want to spend any time with these people because they bring us down, and yet that's our biggest opportunity for transformation.

I believe Rick Warren's book, *The Purpose Driven Life*, is a life-transforming book, and it sets forth the values I live my life by. The first sentence in the book is "It's not about you." And that's the starting point in a person's servant leadership transformation: "It's not about me." This is true whether a person is agnostic, atheist, Christian, Muslim, Buddhist, Hindu, or any other religion. It doesn't make a difference to us what religious beliefs people have, as long as they understand our mission and purpose and they want to help people. For most, it's an adjustment to how they think and how they've been trained in their culture. We have a young Muslim who works for us; and whenever we go through a door together, he will not let me open the door for him. He always says, "You go first, sir." That's just the way he was trained in his culture. I tease him about it now. When we get to a door, I'll say, "Okay, I'm going to get the door this time." He'll say, "No sir, no sir, no sir, no sir, no sir." We're a team; we just have a different set of beliefs when it comes to his letting me help him because of his culture and what he believes. And there's nothing wrong with that. But I do put my foot down when he wants to call me Mr. Barter. If anyone calls me Mr. Barter, I turn around and look for my dad. I want to be called Art.

Businesses Must Create Results

No matter how well a company implements the servant leadership culture—by creating the safe environment, forming the small groups, and helping people transform their hearts and behaviors—the requirement to produce results will always be there. People still have to service the customers and make deliveries on time. They can't just take time off to develop a servant leadership culture and not worry about the way the business is going. You can train people to be great servant leaders, but if you don't combine that with results, you will have a company that is not going to be around very long.

What we've seen, though, is that the companies that do implement servant leadership see great results. Most businesses track some kind of metrics, whether it's financial, operational, customer satisfaction, or whatever is important to their business. When we're helping a consulting client implement servant leadership, we ask them to pick one or two metrics they are currently measuring, and we watch those metrics to see if they improve after their investment into changing the culture. Because servant leadership is a better way to lead, they never fail to see improvements in most of their metrics.

For Datron, our biggest improvement came in being able to do a lot more with the same amount of people. Our productivity went up across the board. At one time people were telling us that when we hit $50 to $55 million in revenue, we would have to upgrade the management team with leaders who had experience running that size company. What we discovered, though, is that because we had created an environment that was all about teamwork and working together to help the people beside you, we were able to do more without adding on a lot of people or changing our management team.

When we moved into our eighty-thousand-square-foot building here in Vista, we thought it was a great place for growth. However, in our limiting belief, we thought that our capacity to produce was only $30–40 million max—about double what we were doing when we moved in. Imagine our delight several years later when we were able to produce $175 million in products from that same building. Our servant leadership culture had enabled us to not only reduce the amount of labor that goes into building our products, but also to increase our efficiency. We saw amazing capability from our people on the production floor as they were building the products our customers needed, and we were able to blow our production out of the water.

Part of the productivity metric is headcount. I think our biggest surprise in all this was the amount of work we were able to do with less people. We knew we could increase our productivity some, but the amount of work our people were actually able to do was unbelievable.

Our productivity wasn't the only metric we saw a significant increase in after we launched servant leadership. As we were growing, we hit record revenues, record profits, and record cash flow. Our gross margin went through the roof. We focused on our gross margin—what it costs to generate a product for a revenue dollar, which includes our materials, labor, and overhead expenses. We now generally achieve somewhere between a 30 and 40 percent gross margin. We get pretty competitive at times, and we may have to work to increase our margin. But that margin is what allows us to increase the money we're now able to reinvest in engineering, in more sales people, and in marketing and trade shows—all the things that help us maintain the health of the company. And remember that we have not borrowed any money to do any of this. It has all been internally funded, because we were able to maintain our high margins.

As you might guess, it's not always rosy when it comes to financial metrics. There have been years when we've had to pull back because our revenue went down. Because we're a private company, we don't care about the quarter-to-quarter revenues. We just care about serving our customers. Lower revenue is not a failure in our eyes, because in our mindset we measure success in the influence we have in the marketplace and those we help; to my knowledge, we've never experienced loss there.

When we decided to launch into servant leadership, we didn't change any of the financial metrics we looked at or any of our financial reporting. The one thing we did change was that we started sharing that information every quarter with everyone in the company. The entire management team now sees the same financial statements and results I see each month, and then once a quarter I share that information with everyone in the organization in an all-hands meeting. A lot of companies create a presentation for employees and shareholders with a bit of their spin in it. But our approach is to show the numbers and then talk about why we didn't get the results we were shooting for (if that is the case). And then we go a step further. We talk about the initiatives we've established to improve those results.

One company we know has seen some gains across most of their financial metrics, but the main thing they measure is engagement and service. They are one of the largest providers of post-acute care in settings that range from transitional care hospitals to home health services, so a lot of their work is in the senior environment. When they get a new patient, the situation has often already progressed to the point where the family is discouraged. They're usually not sure what the future holds for the patient or even how much longer he or she will survive. They are faced day in and day out with situations where people are dealing with serious life events.

I was fortunate enough to be at a conference and heard one of their amazing stories about what they do above and beyond just financials results. They shared stories about some of the successes they were seeing, and one was about a patient they had received who was pretty ill. In fact, his family didn't believe he would ever get well, and neither did he. His daughter was getting married within a short period of time after he was admitted, so someone on staff who was helping with his care asked his daughter to bring in the shoes he was supposed to wear for her wedding. The caretaker put those shoes on his feet every single day, reaffirming each day that he would be at his daughter's wedding. It changed his mindset, and he made it to the wedding. What matters most to them is not necessarily their gains in financial metrics—it's that engagement between their employees and their patients. Their customer satisfaction is going through the roof.

There is another metric we use, and we believe it is the most telling in measuring the impact of the servant leadership culture. We call it our trust index. In a trusting environment, the team is really dedicated to getting great results together. In a team that has a high trust index, people celebrate and have fun together. There is more opportunity for people to grow, things get done faster, and costs go down. When people feel good about themselves and the company they work for, they're going to out-perform all expectations.

Here's how we measure trust in our company. We ask everyone in the company two questions every six months: 1) Do you trust your boss—yes or no? 2) Do you trust management—yes or no? We got those two questions from Stephen M. R. Covey's book, *The Speed of Trust*. Here's what he says about this survey in his book: "I know of leading organizations who ask their employees directly the following simple question in formal, 360-degree feedback processes: *'Do you trust your boss?'* These companies have learned that the answer to this one question is more predictive of team and organizational performance than any other question they might ask."

When we took that survey the first time, we passed out a sheet of paper with just those two questions and asked our people to check off the box on each question—yes or no. One of our employees on the production floor stood up and asked, "Art, who is management?" I said, "Well, that's interesting. We have a different kind of problem here. Before we can measure trust, we need to show you who management is." I asked everyone in the company who had the title of manager or above to come up to the front of the room, and I said, "This is your management team. Do you trust this team? Yes or no?" Then someone else asked, "What if you trust some of them but don't trust others?" I said, "Then the answer is no. You have to trust all of them." We got those results, but we decided that before we would look at them, we would ask another question to just those on the management team: "Do you trust each other? Yes or no." The first time we took that survey, the lowest trust index came from the management team. It turns out that we didn't trust each other.

So the takeaway for me was that I needed to improve the trust index on the management team first, before I asked them to go out and earn the trust of their people. We have brought in Stephen M. R. Covey on several occasions, because he has some great tools to help us improve our trust index. He also speaks at our conferences, which our people are required to attend, so they get Stephen's teachings a couple of times a year.

When we started our study of trust, one of the things we wanted to accomplish was for our management team to be comfortable with having people respond to those questions with a show of hands. We didn't want the vote to be on paper. And taking it one step further, we wanted the management team to be comfortable with having those who voted *no* tell us—in front of the whole group—what they needed in order to improve that trust so they could answer *yes*. It took a little while, but we finally got there. Our last trust rating of the management team was 100 percent *yes*. I've included detailed results from our trust survey over the years in the appendix.

We've also been teaching our leaders to extend trust—to not hold back and wait for someone to earn their trust, but to extend that trust until it is violated. I think that training has really started to take hold because people trust the leaders more when they see that their leaders extend trust to them.

Educate, Understand, Apply, and Reflect

We mentioned in Chapter Two that the ideal servant leadership transformational cycle starts with education. The first thing you do in the cycle is learn. Then you come to understand what you've learned and how it might be integrated into your life. Then you apply what you've learned and set some goals or some initiatives—some things you want to improve. And finally you reflect on yourself and the results and how you have improved. And then you start the process all over again, saying, "I want to get better in these three or four areas." You start to learn again, and then understand how that learning is going to apply to your life and your organization, and then you set goals again, and then you look at the results and reflect.

Servant leadership's a continuous cycle of learning, understanding, improving on your goals, and reflecting. In the reflecting part of the cycle, we measure where we've been against where we want to go so we will know what we still need to work on in the other three areas. We will never know all there is to know or achieve 100 percent excellence in all we do, but the journey is far better—and produces far more satisfying results—than anything else out there. The potential for a higher level of influence on our world is the one thing about servant leadership that is immeasurable.

In early 2017, I published *The Servant Leadership Journal*, an eighteen-week journey to transform you and your organization. From it, I've included the Introduction and Chapter One, titled Intentional Servant Leadership, in the Appendix. I would encourage you and your team to read this excerpt before answering the Chapter Four Table Talk Questions.

PERSONAL	TEAM
1. Do you convey to those you lead that it's safe to fail?	1. Has your team created an environment where your people feel safe to fail?
2. How well do you work as part of the flock?	2. How well does your team work together like a flock of geese?
3. Describe a time when you had a positive experience in your servant leadership transformation and a time when you struggled.	3. Have your team share in a group format about their positive experiences in their transformations, as well as their struggles.
4. Is your life all about you, or is it about helping others?	4. Does your team maintain an "all about me" or and "all about others" attitude?
5. How is your trust index with those who report to you?	5. How is the trust index within and outside of your team?
6. Think about the cycle of learning and measure where you've been against where you want to go.	6. Think about the cycle of learning and measure where your team has been against where you want to go.
7. What do you need to improve?	7. What does your team need to improve?

_____

_____

_____

_____

_____

_____

_____

Chapter Four Table Top Questions

5

Reflection: Business Reviews of a Different Nature

The Guy in the Glass
By Peter Dale Wimbrow, Sr.

When you get what you want in your struggle for pelf*
And the world makes you king for a day
Then go to the mirror and look at yourself
And see what that guy has to say.

For it isn't your father, or mother, or wife
Whose judgment upon you must pass
The feller whose verdict counts most in your life
Is the guy staring back from the glass.

He's the feller to please—never mind all the rest
For he's with you, clear up to the end
And you've passed your most dangerous, difficult test
If the guy in the glass is your friend.

You can fool the whole world down the pathway of years
And get pats on the back as you pass
But your final reward will be heartaches and tears
If you've cheated the guy in the glass.

(*Money, riches)

After my parents passed away within a few months of each other several years ago, I found this poem among their possessions. It was typed on a brown sheet of paper, obviously from an old typewriter. I thought perhaps my grandfather had written it, since he was a minister and enjoyed writing; or that it could have been written by my great aunt, who was an English teacher. But our research revealed that it was written in 1934 by Peter Dale Wimbrow, Sr., who was an American composer, radio artist, and writer. (Actually, the poem I found was entitled "The Man in the Glass" and a few of the words were different. The original poem, as written by Mr. Wimbrow, also had an additional verse. In an effort to correct the inaccuracies widely associated with the poem, his children established a website, www.theguyintheglass.com. They were very proud of their father and wanted to provide this poem as it was actually written for any and all to use as his gift to the world. An interesting tidbit we found on their website is that many people have claimed authorship of this poem over the years—falsely taking credit for a poem about being honest with yourself! It makes you wonder what the guy in their glass had to say about that!)[7]

Key Reflection Traits

Both self-reflection and team reflection are integral elements of the servant leadership culture. The management team at Datron gets together often to discuss where we are in the business. Sometimes we might have a weekly review on a project, but most of the time we get together once a month for lunch and talk about where we are and what's going on. Then once a quarter we go off-site for a two-day meeting. During these business reviews, my role is that of a facilitator as I try to get the best out of my team.

As "The Guy in the Glass" poem says, reflection has to start with ourselves. I go back to it often, because it has a great message: I can fool a lot of people, but I can't fool the guy in the mirror. As a leader, I have to be honest with myself. Before these business reviews, I ask myself these questions:

---

7   Dale Wimbrow, The Official Guy in the Glass Web Page, http://www.theguyinthe-glass.com (accessed 12/2/15).

What am I doing to help the team?

Where am I adding value to the team?

How am I detracting from the team?

How am I not having a positive impact on the team?

I look at those things first and see how I can improve personally. Then while we're conducting these business reviews, if I get a response I didn't expect, I ask myself another question:

What did I do to generate that response?

After you look at yourself first, then you have to be honest and embrace reality about your leadership team:

Where are we in our maturity and transformation?

Are we able to get results?

How effective are we as a management team?

Do we have any silos in the organization?

How is the team working across department lines? Are any of our teams more in tune with themselves than they are with the other teams in the organization?

You also have to be honest about your results. When I came up through the corporate world, I spent more time trying to determine how to spin the results and make them look better than actually addressing what was causing the problem. A servant leader must be straightforward and honest about the results you're getting and basically stay in what we call the "no-spin zone." You're either on track or you're not.

In our business reviews, we use what we call a "one-page plan." That one-page plan has our values, mission, and purpose at the top to remind us why we're doing what we're doing. Then it lists our revenue and profit goals for the next four quarters. Next are the top five or six goals we want to accomplish for the year, and then we list two or three goals we want to accomplish in the next ninety days. Every box below that is a departmental box that each department puts together to support the ninety-day plan and the one-year forecast.

At the end of each quarter, we review the goals and code each goal's results with a color indicator. Blue means we're getting awesome results; green means we're getting the results we expected; yellow means we didn't achieve the results we wanted, but we're at least moving forward; and red means we didn't meet the target and we really need to look at this goal right away because there's danger here.

After reflecting on how you, personally, and your team can improve, the next step is to create what I call "a fascination for the truth." Let's say you look at your results for the quarter and you didn't meet your goals. Now you need to say, "I want to hear everything that's truthful about why we didn't meet this goal and look at what didn't work." This is where it's critical that you have a safe environment so people will open up and talk about their challenges and why they fell short. If your people know you have a fascination for the truth, it's much easier for them to open up.

So how do we create this fascination-for-the-truth environment? The first thing I have to do as a leader is assure my people they will not be punished for telling me the truth—whatever it is. That means I must be retrained in my response to the truth. Sometimes the truth is that a decision I made didn't work, and I want my people to know they can tell me that. Also, since my family works here in the business with me, I have to be open to the truth about whether my daughter and son are performing the way they should be. I've always told the leaders in my organization who have had my daughter or son working for them that they need to treat them just like any other employee; and if they don't, that's when they're going to be mentored by the CEO. When you have a fascination for the truth, you have to create a culture where it's okay to tell the boss he's wrong and where it's okay to say, "I made a mistake."

Monthly Management Team Investments

Once a month, we invest two hours in a lunch for the management team, when we get together and talk about what's going on in the business. We often bring in people from outside the company to speak during these lunches. Several months ago we brought in an expert in workplace violence prevention to help the team understand what bullying in the workplace looks like and how to anticipate workplace violence. (One of the really interesting things he told us is that anger toward objects is a step away from workplace violence. When someone throws things, slams doors, or slams down a phone, he or she could potentially be a step away from a violent situation.) Sometimes we bring in a video to watch, such as one of Ken Blanchard's videos on leadership. And sometimes we bring in a speaker from the community. We look at that monthly luncheon as an investment into our management team. Part of my job is to add value to the team, and sometimes that involves my paying someone to come in and talk to us. From time to time, though, we just get together to share a lunch, with no agenda and no discussion about business; we just want to hang out together. I actually do that with my senior team every week—we go to lunch just to spend time together, with no meeting and no agenda.

Quarterly Management Team Off-sites

Every quarter, usually within thirty days after our quarter ends, we bring in all our leaders who are based in the US for a two-day off-site meeting. The first morning is usually spent sharing results. Our CFO takes us through our profit and loss statement, our balance sheet, and our cash flow statement. The team gets to see the same numbers I see, the actual numbers for the quarter. Then we go through all of the goals on our one-page plan that we said we were going to do in ninety days, and we let the team determine the ranking on how we did and assign a color to each one. It's a team decision—not mine or any other individual's. The team ranks itself on its own performance.

Then we take a break, go make copies of the one-page plan

for everyone, and come back to do an in-depth review of the goals. We celebrate the greens and the blues, where we did well and where we did awesome. Then we dig into the reds and the yellows in detail. We ask, "Why are we red in these areas? What's going on there? What do we need to do to improve and what does that department need from this leadership team to help it get back on track? Do we need to change the goal, or is it still valid?" We challenge ourselves on every red and yellow goal. Then we decide if that item needs to stay on our goals for the next ninety days. Most of the time the reds and yellows stay on the report, and the greens and blues—the ones we accomplished—come off.

When we're looking at the reds and the yellows, we really get into that fascination for the truth about why we didn't meet those goals. Let me give you an example: Last quarter we missed our booking goal (new orders) by a pretty big amount. A $30-million order was moved out of the quarter into a future time. So we talked about what we knew about this order and what we should have known about this order. Did we have the right intelligence about the status of the order? Were we talking to the right people about where the order was? Were we expecting something that, deep down, we knew wasn't going to happen? We challenged ourselves on every point about why the order was pushed out of the quarter. Then we talked about what we were going to do differently on orders that were forecast for the next six months and how we were going to apply what we learned.

Then we talk about the yellows—those goals we made progress on but are not where we wanted to be. We talk about how we can speed up the timelines to get them done quicker. We ask ourselves, "Have we set the right priorities? Do we have the right resources allocated?" And again, we go back to the fascination about the truth and ask why we weren't able to make the progress we thought we could ninety days before.

Then we start the process of re-setting our one-page plan for the next quarter. That might involve a group discussion where we stay together as a team, or it might be that the management team needs to break up into subgroups that go off and work on specific items. It all depends on what the challenges are. We often have them focus on one area to determine what's going on, and that's when we may have some really challenging conversations. We call them "courageous conversations," where people challenge each other so we can get to the truth about what's taking place. That's when you find out how dedicated your leaders are about getting down to the true specifics. You will have some leaders who are seriously fascinated with the truth, and other leaders who like to make general comments that don't create any commitments on their part. It can produce some good, challenging conversations.

As the leader facilitating all of this, I have to really watch my own attitude and actions. I've discovered over the years that when I, as the CEO, get passionate about something (which is a nice way of saying that I'm upset), it shuts my team down. Let's say we don't agree with where a conversation is going on a certain subject, or don't think the team is really addressing reality, or think they're not taking action fast enough on something that needs to be done quickly. If I get too excited and jump in and force my opinion into the conversation, my team shuts down and I won't get anything out of them for the rest of the day.

In a recent quarterly off-site meeting, I broke my own rule and got excited about a subject we were discussing. When we took a break, I borrowed a toy yellow duck that one of our employees had on her desk and brought it back into the meeting with me. I told the team, "I'm going to make a new rule for myself for the rest of the meeting." I said, "Here's the rule: Since I couldn't keep my emotions under control in our last session, I can now only talk when I have the duck in my hand," and I gave the duck to one of my senior leaders. I knew I had to show my team that I was going to hold myself accountable by letting them decide when I could talk and when I couldn't. That kept the conversation going in the right direction so we could have an open discussion. This is a good example of giving the power you have over to your team. I gave the power of my lips to my team and let them determine when I could talk.

Investing Money into Developing Your Team

If you're serious about developing your leaders and you want to help them grow into positions where they can take on greater responsibility and reach their goals, you have to invest in their development. At Datron, we have implemented several programs to aid in the development of our leaders.

First, we require our management team to read books on leadership and organizational development. In the past we asked them to read two books a year. This year, though, we decided that since the market is moving so fast, we all really need to be reading one book every three months. The Leadership Council selects the books, and we pay for them. It's an investment, but one we believe is essential for our growth.

We also encourage our management team to go to two servant leadership conferences a year—one of the Servant Leadership Institute conferences and one that's not related to the company, so they will get some outside influence in leadership.

But the biggest and most impactful investment we make is giving our people access to some of the best leadership development minds in the country. We are considered a small company by most standards. But in spite of our size we are dedicated to paying the price to bring in the best people we can find, like John Maxwell, Ken Blanchard, Stephen M. R. Covey, and John Izzo, to help in the development of our leaders. They dedicate an entire day to working directly with our team, on-site. In order to be able to afford them, we get creative; for example, we discovered that we could afford John Maxwell if we negotiated a three-year deal with him to come and be with us twice a year. You can imagine the impact John Maxwell can make when he spends time with just thirty to thirty-five leaders, as opposed to speaking to an audience of thousands. We brought in Stephen

M. R. Covey this year to help us with trust. Yes, these leadership experts are expensive, but the payback we get in growing our leaders is unbelievable.

After a couple of years of bringing these experts in, we realized that we could double the impact of our investment if we had them spend the morning session developing the management team and then spend the afternoon session impacting the husband and wife teams. Since we have always believed that the spouses have a lot to do with our success—with their support, patience, and understanding—we like to give back to them by asking these leaders to do something that will enhance the relationship between spouses. When we first started that, we had no idea what we were getting into. These experts have helped a lot of people—including me and Lori—grow exponentially in their marriage relationship. You may remember from Chapter Two the exercise I mentioned that John Izzo did with the team and our spouses about the five most important things we want to do before we die. It was powerful and life-changing—probably the most intense afternoon the team has ever had.

Yes, it costs a lot of money, dollar-for-dollar, to bring these experts in; but what you get from them is priceless. Go ahead and make the investment. Don't be afraid to call someone and say, "Can you make an introduction? I'd like to figure out how I can engage them to come talk to my team."

I keep a file called Why We Do What We Do. It is a file where I keep the cards and notes that I received from those that we've invested in and served over the years. It is a great file to go through when you are down, a great pick me up, but what I like most about the file is it reminds me to live my life for the sake of others. It is truly worth the effort. The investment you make in people—in your employee's when done with the right motive—returns stories that will last you a lifetime. I would like to share with you several of those stories.

The following was written by an employee who I first met when she applied at Datron to be my executive assistant. We had just completed the purchase of Datron and I was interviewing candidates for the position. She was currently working in a legal firm in downtown San Diego. She was looking for something different, but I would find out after hiring her that she wasn't really sure what she wanted to do. She just knew there had to be something different and hopefully better in life. She met with me at our manufacturing facility in Vista, quite a difference from the environment she was used to. I learned that she had had second thoughts about the interview when she sat in our lobby comparing her current higher-end office building to our economical manufacturing environment. But she didn't judge us on our appearance and ended up accepting my offer to join the Datron family as my executive assistant. I helped her figure out what she wanted to do, provided her support through our educational reimbursement program to obtain a higher-level degree, all in support of her dream to use her gifts in her job. After she obtained her new Executive MBA, I knew she would not be happy long term as my assistant, so I provided her an opportunity in a staff position as director of operational and strategic planning. In her new role, she did not have any staff reporting to her; she was required to work in the Datron open matrix organization. In 2010 I received this note in a Christmas card:

> Art, I've composed this card in my head all year long. In March, I was going to thank you for including Nasir and I as guests at the Monarch benefit, recount the days I spent in February for the Blanchard EMBA alumni conference, and thank you for advising me to buy a diary for my trip to India! In June, I would have added diary entries from my family reunion trip to Texas and the opportunity to see Jim Collins speak at the CEN conference in Colorado. By September, I would be remembering to thank you for the opportunity to speak at the Active Strategy conference in Philadelphia and travel to Atlanta to copresent at the

Greenleaf conference. Now it's December already and I can include seeing Covey and Maxwell in Maui, taking part in building the technology roadmap in Florida, and presenting at the Palladium conference in San Diego. The gifts you've given me are too numerous to account on this bit of paper but know that, because of your trust in me, I have grown by an immeasurable amount and I will treasure these gifts always. Thank you from the bottom of my heart for your continued faith and council. Merry Christmas!

This is why we do what we do, to invest in lives so they grow through transformation to their full potential.

Sometime in 2013, I received a note from another employee for a different reason. Our company rented a car for her and her husband to use while they saved enough money to buy a new one. They were newlyweds and both Lori and I could relate to their struggles just as we did when we were first married. We decided to help them out with a rental car. This was a note of thanks we received from them.

Art and Lori, Thank you for coming to our rescue by providing me with a safe car while we save for the next one. I was overwhelmed with appreciation and both Alex and I truly feel cared for and abundantly supported by you both. I know you didn't feel obligated to gift us in this way, it's just who you are!! Wow, and the rental doesn't break down on us every other week. Thank you for blessing us!

Her husband wrote in the same card the following:

Thank you so much for the swift and overwhelming response to our car problems. It's such a relief to know we can make it to work each day and it's just another reminder of how much you've blessed us. We appreciate it deeply! Thank you!

Our investment at times revolves around meeting the basic needs of others. At times, those you've invested in may decide to accept an offer from another company, which this employee did. In April 2015, on her last day at the company, she wrote Lori and I the following in a card:

> I want to thank you for the opportunity to serve alongside you these past five years at SLI. My eyes have been opened, my thinking has been shifted for the better and I've experienced real, honest, unforgettable growth here through your beliefs and investment in servant leadership. I feel as though I will always have family here so I especially thank you for your cultivating a culture that looks out for one another, encourages (sometimes teases), but always supports and loves. Because of this experience I am forever changed, unwilling to accept the status quo and always looking for opportunities to use my influence to serve and make a difference in any community I'm a part of. So thank you for inspiring that in me. This frame gift contains our first-ever servant leadership conference. I smile when I look at it because I'm reminded of how far SLI has come, how far the conference has come, and to remind you that it all started with an idea, after you had a change in mindset and a strong tugging on your heart. In those five years, you've managed to impact so many people through the conference and other SLI activities. And I know from the depths of my heart that you are only going to impact many more! Thank you.

We were sad to see her go, but reminded ourselves through the process that our job as servant leaders is to help people grow and get better. There are no limitations on that growth, nor do we put constraints on our investment in others that require them to stay with the company to grow. We celebrated her growth and job offer. At the same time, I wrote a letter to the CEO of the company she was joining passing

ART BARTER

on responsibility for this young leader's life to them. Do those you serve grow? And when they have an opportunity to grow with another company, do we stand in the way or let them go? Servant Leaders let lives grow wherever the opportunity is.

The last note I would like to share with you comes from an employee who is currently part of the SLI team and wrote this note to me and Lori in 2017:

> Dear Art and Lori,
>
> I wanted to take a moment to thank you for everything you have done and are continuing to do for my family and I. Not only by employing me at a truly unique and amazing company, but also by providing me with the opportunity to go back to school and better myself and therefore my family. Thank you for the grant you have in place at Mira Costa College as it is truly helping me to have an easier time with being back in school, and it enables me to continue going to school and bettering myself with education. You are such an inspiration to me and I truly value everything that I have learned this past two-and-a-half years with SLI. And I wanted to make sure to take the time to make sure you knew the impact you're having on me. Servant leadership and all its teachings so truly transform my entire life, from the way I think, to the way I choose to react in all areas of my life. It's made me a better employee, mother, student, partner, friend and overall person and I truly hope to impact someone's life the way you and the people who surround you are continually impacting mine. Thank you for everything, and I pray to continue to be a source of support that is used to help inspire and equip everyone I come across, much like you and your family have done for me. Your generosity, grace, and sincerity and true servant leader's heart shines through in your actions and behaviors, and I am grateful to be part of it. Sincerely yours in service.

Invest in other lives. The journey you will witness and be part of is priceless, and it will make you a better person and better leader.

Keeping Yourself Healthy

As a leader, you are responsible for a lot of lives, so you really have to make sure you understand where you are with your health. Like many other busy CEOs, I fell into the trap of believing I was invincible. I had plenty of warning signs that something wasn't right with my health, but because I had the wrong mindset I did nothing to change my lifestyle.

In 2013, the weekend before our annual SLI conference was to start, I didn't feel well. I was scheduled to host a reception on Monday evening, so I decided to go to the doctor Monday morning. Lori went with me, which she normally doesn't do. As it turned out, it was a good thing she did. When I went in to see the doctor, I had in mind that he would give me a magic pill so I could get through the reception that night and through the next two days of the conference. Then I would have time to take care of myself after the conference.

The nurse took my blood pressure and my temperature, and when the doctor came in he said, "You have 104 temperature. You're going to the hospital." I said, "Okay," but I was thinking, *I have to figure out a way to get down to the hotel, because I'm hosting a reception tonight.* The doctor asked me if I wanted to go in my car or in an ambulance. I thought, *if I go in an ambulance I'll be handled more quickly as an emergency. I'll get the magic pill from the doctor at the hospital, and I'll still be able to make the reception.* So we jumped into the ambulance and headed to the hospital. When we got there, of course the hospital emergency room was packed; they didn't have a room for me, so I laid on a gurney in a hallway for about twenty or thirty minutes. The entire time I was lying there I was thinking, *I have to get going. I have to get down to the reception. I have to get going. I have to get the magic pill.*

Lori says I was awake, but I don't remember being wheeled

into a room or anything after that. The next thing I remember is waking up on Thursday morning. I told Lori, "The conference is starting today. We have to get down to the conference!" She said, "Honey, the conference is over." I said, "No, it's Tuesday morning." "No, it's Thursday morning," she told me. That's when I started to realize I was seriously ill. All the way up to that time, going into the hospital, lying on that gurney, I was looking for the magic pill so I could go do my work.

At that time I weighed 470 pounds. The least I had weighed in my adult life was about 210. Right around the time I bought the company, I weighed about 220. With the stress of everything going on then and since then, I failed to take good care of myself, and I piled on the weight. Many people tried to help me, including Ken Blanchard. When I didn't listen to Ken, he sent a doctor to meet me who had lost weight himself. The doctor said, "Here's a copy of my book. I'd love to help you. Read it and give me a call." I never found time to read the book—until I was in the hospital recovering.

While I was in the hospital, the doctors discovered three things: I had an infection that had taken over my abdomen (which, in retrospect, I believe I had had for almost a year), the oxygen level in my blood stream had dropped to around the mid 30s, and I had sleep apnea. My oxygen level should have been about 90 percent. It is a miracle I lived! The doctors believed it was the infection that caused my oxygen level to go so low. While I was still out those first three days, one of the nurses was taking information and she asked Lori, "What does your husband do during the day?" Lori said, "He goes to work." The nurse said, "What do you mean, he goes to work?" Lori said, "Well, he gets up and he drives to the office and goes to work." All the nurses were astounded that I could even function with an oxygen level that low! They couldn't believe that I could even drive to work with as little oxygen as I had, much less work all day!

My son came into my hospital room one day while I was

sleeping and asked the doctor, "What's going on with my dad?" The doctor rattled off a lot of medical jargon, and Chris said, "Could you talk to me in a language I can understand?" The doctor said, "Simply put, here's what's happening: Your dad is sitting in the car in the garage with the car running; there is a garden hose with one end stuck in the tail pipe and the other end stuck through the car window, and he's basically killing himself." Carbon monoxide was taking over my body because I didn't have enough oxygen in my blood stream.

I didn't learn about that conversation until six months after I got out of the hospital. I hated that my son had to go through that. I put my kids and Lori through hell. I had had many people trying to warn me that I needed to take care of myself, and I ignored all of them—and paid the price.

Two weeks into my stay, the hospital was going to discharge me. My ankles were swollen so badly they were huge, and I couldn't walk. The doctors wanted me to go to a nursing home for six weeks, and I said, "No, I'm not going to do that." A good friend who was in the medical field introduced me to a doctor who had dealt with men my size before. He showed up in my hospital room one night about nine o'clock, and he said, "Art, I need to get some of this water out of your system." He explained that when you get to the size I was, your body doesn't know when it's going to get water, so it just holds everything inside. So I transferred to another hospital and went under his care, and in thirteen days he took sixty pounds of water out of my body! He got me started, and I've lost over 180 pounds since then.

I have a different respect for health today, as well as different priorities. I've changed my lifestyle. I haven't been to a fast-food restaurant since I got out of the hospital, and I drink very little of what I call "foo-foo coffee." We can't be good leaders unless we're healthy. I had a company full of people who didn't know if their CEO was going to make it out of the hospital. Leaders owe it to their people to take care of themselves. That's more important than anything else you have to do in your business. It's the most important thing you can do for your family.

Today, I reflect on what I put Lori through. She spent two-and-a-half days by my side not knowing whether I would wake up. I can't take it back, but I can try to make sure she doesn't have to go through that again by taking better care of my health. God has given me talent to influence others in their leadership mindset, a heart to help others, and a desire to live my life in accordance with His will. Being a good steward of those gifts is my responsibility.

How are you doing with that guy in the glass? Is he or she your friend? In the end, that's the only verdict that counts, because...

> You can fool the whole world down the pathway of years
> And get pats on the back as you pass
> But your final reward will be heartaches and tears
> If you've cheated the guy in the glass.

PERSONAL

1. What are you doing to help your team?
2. Where are you adding value to your team?
3. How are you detracting from your team?
4. How are you not having a positive impact on your team?
5. Do you have a fascination for the truth?
6. Are you taking care to stay healthy?
7. How are you doing with that guy in the glass?

TEAM

1. Where is your team in its maturity and transformation?
2. How effective are you as a management team?
3. Is your team able to get results?
4. How is your team working across department lines?
5. Does your team have a fascination for the truth?
6. How does your team invest in the development of its leaders?
7. Does your team encourage each other to stay healthy?

_____

_____

_____

_____

_____

_____

_____

Chapter Five Table Top Questions

6

Living Your Purpose Day to Day

"Being successful and fulfilling your life's purpose are not at all the same thing. You can reach all your personal goals, become a raving success by the world's standard and still miss your purpose in this life."

—Rick Warren

How do you inspire your people to live your company's purpose? According to Christopher J. Nassetta, president and CEO of Hilton Worldwide, "It's really about developing a culture and creating an environment where people feel like they are part of something that is bigger than they are."[8]

The first eight years of my career were spent working in the office at Disneyland, and I was always inspired by their purpose: "We create happiness by providing the finest in entertainment for people of all ages, everywhere." I recently saw on one of Disney's websites that they now call it "the common purpose," rather than "the company purpose." I like that. "Common purpose" indicates a cause that is bigger than any individual or leader; it's a purpose of the whole. It speaks of alignment in purpose and values. It says that it's something they *all* feel passionate about. Their common purpose is some-

---

8   Jeff James, Disney Institute, Talking Point: The Disney Institute Blog, "Common Purpose: How to Inspire Your Staff," https://disneyinstitute.com/blog/2012/09/common-purpose-how-to-inspire-your-staff/100 (accessed 12/10/15).

thing they can dedicate their lives to. It's a noble calling that brings them together.

Datron's purpose is "To positively impact the lives of others, today and in the future." Though we have not called it our "common purpose" in the past, that's exactly what it has been. That's because we have worked hard to develop that culture and create that environment where our people see it as something bigger than themselves.

How Will Your Organization Live the Common Purpose?

If you want the people in your organization to live your purpose, you must lead by example. Your mindset has to be one of constantly living your purpose. If your purpose truly represents the reason for your company's very existence, let it shine through every goal, every strategy, and every activity. Commit to communicating over and over again to your people.

Many of today's emerging leaders are looking for purpose and meaning in their lives. When I entered the workforce with the rest of the boomers, we were looking for job security. If we happened to enjoy what we were doing, that was a major plus. But the leaders who are entering the workforce now really want to find something they know is making a difference in the world. They want to be a part of "something bigger than themselves."

Our SLI team has recently been working with a leading global security company to help them implement servant leadership into their culture. Their vision serves as a beacon to lead their people to that something bigger: "To be the most trusted provider of systems and technologies that insure the security and freedom of our nation and its allies. As the technology leader, we will define the future of defense..." Their purpose incorporates both short-term and long-term goals. The first things you see when you step into their world are helicopters and all kinds of systems with weapons on them. But they don't look at them as weapons of war—they see them as a means to freedom. That's a noble calling for their people, one that is bigger than themselves.

The big challenge comes in communicating your purpose to your people to the point that it becomes a part of their life's purpose. It's not just something you put on your website and in company documents. You have to back it up with behavior and communicate it every day.

Put Your Money Where Your Mouth Is

A lot of companies say they want to change their culture to support their purpose, but they don't back it up with their wallet. One such company told its leaders they could attend our servant leadership training the first whole day on company time, but they would have to take personal time off to attend the second half day. In essence, management was saying, "We're serious about this. However, we're not willing to put our pocketbook behind it quite yet."

Chris Stokes was with us at our SLI conference in Florida recently. He and his brother started the Jamaican bobsled team, and their story was told in the movie *Cool Runnings*. During a question and answer session, one of the leaders who attended asked, "How do I expose my people to this training?" We suggested that he bring some of his people to one of our conferences, and he said, "I can't afford that." So we said, "Maybe not, but you can bring the conference to your people." He came back with, "I don't have the money or the resources to do that." Here is Chris Stokes's response: "I don't understand leadership in America. In Jamaica, we didn't have any money and we didn't have any snow, and yet we entered the winter Olympics in bobsledding."

This made me think: we have such limiting beliefs in what we can do when it comes to training our employees. Leaders are never going to have all the resources they want or need, so we have to teach them to be creative. It all boils down to the priorities they place on those resources. If they want their people to live their common purpose, they're going to have to invest some time and money into making sure they understand and buy into that purpose. They need to change their mindset from seeing their training as an expense to seeing it as an *investment*. They are investing in the future of their people, which will generate a massive return in employee engagement. Part of that return is in low turnover. At Datron, most of our turnover rate is in the Engineering Department. We don't design products with the latest and greatest technology. It's just the nature of our business; when engineers are working with what they would deem average technology and they are offered an opportunity to work at another company that generates cutting-edge technology, they're going to take that opportunity. And we support that, because that's not something we can offer them. That "something bigger" in their lives is creating newer and greater technology for the future. In fact, some companies in the technology world support their purpose by allowing their engineers time to go off to the lab to create new technology that may not be directly related to their business. And sometimes the companies are surprised to find that the technology their engineers are working on can be incorporated into their future systems.

Another way for companies to "put their money where their mouth is" in supporting their purpose is to give back to the communities they do business in. A lot of communities put together incentive packages to entice companies to move there, which may include helping them with the permit process, reducing some of their costs by giving them bonds, or any number of other incentives. The people those companies employ generate a lot of economic benefits to the surrounding communities. I believe companies have a responsibility to take some of their profits and give them back to their communities, where people are helping other people.

Some companies have an annual project that their people devote themselves to. They may adopt a facility or the home of someone in need and go in and redo the landscaping, clean up around the outside, or repair or remodel the house. Other companies buy sponsorships in local school or charity events, where they help pay for some of the costs associated with the events. Sponsorships are a great way to get their company's name out there, but they also say, "We believe in this organization and this event." Other companies allow their people to serve on the boards or committees of the local Chamber of Commerce or charitable organizations, and they give them the opportunity to do that on company time.

Some companies indirectly invest in their communities by investing in their employees. One of the companies we met at our annual Servant Leadership Conference shared with us that their employee education benefit pays up to $35,000 a year to help them get an education! When their leaders told me about it, I said, "Do you realize what you have here? You're cutting edge in this area! I don't know of any other company that's willing to invest $35,000 a year to help you get a degree." That is a win-win-win investment—it not only helps the employee; it also ultimately benefits the community because of that employee's future earning capabilities, and it benefits the company because of that employee's future work capabilities.

Another way to make a huge impact in training your people to support your purpose is to bring in outside help—those I call "subject-matter experts," like John Maxwell, Ken Blanchard, and Stephen M. R. Covey. Remember that global defense company I talked about earlier? Part of their purpose was "to be the most trusted provider of systems and technologies…" How will they do that without bringing in someone to train their people about trust? You have to be careful about what you put in your purpose statement, because you have to back it up with money and behavior. You may think you can't afford to bring leadership giants like these in, but think of the return on your investment! When you bring subject-matter experts into your organization, you will be paid back ten-fold. If you're serious about living your purpose, I encourage you to invest your dollars and make it happen.

The Stories Will Come When You Live Your Purpose

When you start to live your purpose, you will have a huge impact on the individuals in your organization. You will begin to hear stories about individuals becoming better people, and about how that has impacted their families. When mom or dad changes for the better, it affects the family, the workplace, and the community. You will hear people say, "This is what happened when I worked for a company where we all shared a common purpose. I was able to help people by rebuilding part of the community. We were able to sponsor the local sports team or the charity events to show that we really cared about those organizations and the people they helped."

Here are some stories that some of our people have shared over the years about how they have been impacted by living our purpose at Datron:

Gary's Story (as shared in *The Power of a Story* booklet):

As a senior leader in manufacturing at Datron, Gary lived a comfortable life with his wife and family. When he got involved in servant leadership, he started making a significant change in the way he leads. He became much more involved with his people, taking time to visit with his direct reports each week and being very intentional about teaching them the servant leadership behaviors. His employees noticed the big changes in Gary.

But Gary made an even bigger change in his personal life. When people from his church asked him to go on a mission trip to earthquake-devastated Haiti, his first reaction was typical of the old Gary: "Before I agree to go, I need to know the purpose, the task, and the objective of the trip." But because of his training in servant leadership, he knew that those answers weren't really important. What he really needed to do was be a willing servant who saw a need and filled it. The trip to Haiti would mean leaving the comforts of home for ten days and living with the Haitian people with no air-conditioning, very intermittent electricity, and even potential danger since robbers often stole food and supplies at night. Gary shared, "Because of the transformation of my attitude through servant leadership training, I have become much less selfish. Now when I encounter new situations, I don't ask what will be best for me; I look for opportunities to help others. This new perspective made it possible for me to eagerly say. 'Yes, I will go and serve in Haiti.'"

Sarah's Story (as shared in the *Culture Transformation* booklet):

Sarah, a member of our Manufacturing Engineering group at Datron and a native of Vietnam, has obtained grants from our Charitable Fund to help the elderly in Vietnam. This past year she requested charitable funds to rebuild an elementary school in her homeland; the granting of these funds gave immense purpose to her work beyond just making a profit.

> ...Without knowing servant leadership, I couldn't be me now. My heart grew bigger and stronger than I was six years ago. I remembered when I first attended the Servant Leadership Level 1, I was asked to share with a group about myself. I was stuck and speechless. I asked myself who I was, what I was good at, and what values I lived with. The training taught me how to reflect myself, to know my values, and the important thing was how to get out of my shell. I was a great and helpful person in my family, but I wasn't a great person in the community. I have learned how to use my values to serve others. In 2008, I was able to reach out to thirty-five needy people and now in 2013 I've reached out and touched more than eight hundred people in the community and in my homeland. Servant leadership not only helped me become a servant leader but also helped me become a person with a servant's heart, and thanks to Art; he influenced me in so many positive ways. Under his great vision and mission...I believe that I have influenced people around me...

After the release of *Farmer Able* I received a request from Diana Aaron, Datron's charitable fund director, to give a signed copy of *Farmer Able* to the Rising Star students in the Vista Unified School District. The program is run by the Vista Chamber of Commerce and recognizes Rising Star students each month at a breakfast. Each month she gives me the list of students that are being recognized. I personalize the book to them by name and write "Congratulations on being a Rising Star! Keep up the great work!" Then I sign each book. Diana attends the breakfast and presents the signed books to the students as recognition for their achievement. Each month I receive thank you notes from each of the students, thanking us for providing the breakfast and the books. Turns out *Farmer Able* is a book for all ages! We were thrilled at the response to the book from the students. Sarah added to our excitement when we discovered a picture on her Facebook page of her and her daughter reading *Farmer Able* together.

> By practicing Servant Leadership, I have inspired my dear family members. For example, my daughter Caroline has been deeply touched by all my hard work. Recently, she made a presentation in class on how she was inspired by my leadership. She had watched a

Servant Leadership video, which included a mini video about how I helped the people in Vietnam, and she presented clips of the mini video to her classmates. I was very moved and so proud of her.

Thanks, Datron, for leading me the right way, with a servant's heart. Not only have you taught me to help others, but now my daughter has been inspired to follow in my footsteps by volunteering with me at Feeding America. Hopefully, she can expand on what she knows and reach out in bigger causes.

Al's Story:

Servant leadership training at Datron helped me lay a foundation for discovering who I am and what my purpose is; you could say it was the road for my journey. I retained bits and pieces of each of the three levels of training. However, in Level One there was a message that I felt was particularly important to me: "People don't care how much you know until they know how much you care." It's an important message because it illustrates that it's not about me, but about others. Each day we have an opportunity to influence other people, and hopefully that will be in a positive way. Don't get me wrong; I have had my moments (you can ask my wife) when I was not on my best behavior. However, Servant Leadership training has taught me to be more aware of my actions. *What did I say or do that did not reflect a serving heart? What was my intention?* The Servant Leadership sessions and books are great, but the most important thing is the actions we take as a result of what we've learned. As the saying goes, "Actions speak louder than words."

Success versus Significance

When I was in my mid-twenties and just getting into the workforce, my dream was to live on Newport Bay, Orange

County, California with a fifty-foot yacht anchored at the dock in front of my house. I wanted to have all that by the time I was forty and then retire. That's what I considered success because that's what everyone was talking about when I was in college. "Where are you going to live? What are you going to own? What kind of car are you going to have? Are you going to have a boat?" So that's what my dream was for many years. I thought I would be successful when I owned nice homes, drove nice cars, dressed nice, and went out to nice restaurants. In my first job as a controller, I was allowed to pick out my own company car and all the options I wanted on it. When it was delivered, I thought, *This is really what success is all about. I'm on my road to success. I'm going to be on that bay by the time I'm forty.*

That's what I wanted, but I had no idea how I was going to get there. I didn't focus on other people; I focused on myself. No one ever sat me down and asked, "Do you really want to be successful in life, with everything about you? Or do you want to be significant and focus on helping other people?"

Significance comes from impacting the lives of other people; so if you want to live a life of significance, you have to think about serving others first. At some point in my career, I started to realize that the dream I was chasing wasn't going to happen. And I recognized that my dream really needed to change; there was no happiness in it. I was not finding joy in my life. I was not finding the purpose I wanted.

The interesting thing is, I was brought up in a household of people helping other people. We lived in a middle class home in Tustin, California. My father worked for the phone company and was responsible for the outlying phone switching stations. My mother stayed at home until all of the kids were in high school and then she went to work for the City of Tustin as their receptionist. I have three sisters, one older and two younger. We grew up in a four bedroom home in a tract neighborhood. I was always out helping my dad in the garage, building something, fixing something, or working on our cars. I had daily chores in the summertime. I had to spend one hour per day working in the yard. When my dad came home at night we walked through the yard and he inspected my work, or at times the lack of my work. He always held me accountable to do what he asked me to do.

My dad belonged to service organizations and churches where he was always helping someone. He never said no when he saw someone with a need. My mom's gift was hospitality; she was always inviting people over to the house, providing them with good food and a caring environment where everyone enjoyed each other's fellowship and just spending time together.

Even though I was raised in that environment, I left school thinking about myself instead of other people. And I didn't even recognize my heritage until I was in my late forties or early fifties.

Obviously, I missed my goal of retiring by the time I was forty; I didn't even come close. About that time, I left the job I had been working at because I was frustrated and wasn't getting anywhere. I just couldn't seem to get to the next level in the company. So I left and went to work for a very small private company in Irvine that made floppy diskettes for computers. That's when I really began to think about my life. My son was born when I was thirty-two, and I believe my priorities in life had started changing then. But it really didn't begin to sink in until I was in my mid to late forties that I wanted to do something different; I wanted to be happy. I was working in an international business that was doing a lot of good, but I didn't realize at the time the impact we were having on people. I spent several years searching for something different, but I didn't know what it was.

My pastor often says, "I can't preach it unless I live it." I've always wondered, *What does he mean by that?* But today I realize that most of the things I teach in leadership, I've lived through; I'm just sharing my experiences. I have the opportunity to help somebody else through these things in a real way because I've lived them.

A key point in the transformation of my life came on

9/11. That was when Lori and I started thinking that we really needed to reintroduce God into our lives. Our faith has probably had the biggest impact on the change in our thinking. Around that time we also had two teenagers in the house; and anyone who has had teenagers will understand when I say that the experiences you have during those years can certainly help you change your mindset!

In 2003, Ken Blanchard entered my life when he came and spoke at my church and challenged my leadership style. He asked a very simple question: "Do you really believe what you believe?" Then he said, "If you're a person of faith and you believe what you believe, then you have to be a servant leader. It's not an option." That was the first time I'd been challenged in my faith. I have a great church and a great pastor who is really focused on teaching from the Bible, and all the men's groups I was involved in were focused on what our faith is all about. But Ken was the one who really bridged my faith to my personal life outside the church building. Once he did that, I came across John Maxwell's Leadership Bible, and that was a continuation of the bridge that helped me take what was said in the Bible and apply it to the real world. John goes through every verse in every chapter to see what God said about leaders and leadership and explains what they mean. He might take something Moses said or something Daniel did and talk about how they apply to leadership. It's like a playbook to me now, because I can look up something like conflict or encouragement and find the verses that apply, and they're translated into today's terms in leadership. That has had a huge impact on relating to my everyday life what I was learning in the Bible.

A note about my faith. I believe my relationship with God is personal. My faith teaches me to accept all people, that we are not to judge others and we serve those placed in front of us. At Datron, I tell others I am not here to evangelize to others; that's not a gift I have been given. Our purpose at Datron is to positively impact the lives of others. There are no religious requirements to help others, and that is why everyone is accepted at Datron. The common purpose we have is our desire to help others.

As I was reflecting on success versus significance, I realized that we have short memories. Sometimes we forget the lessons we've learned and too easily slip back into old ways of behavior. I learned something earlier this year that really helps me remember the behaviors I want to engage in every day to be significant. It's actually a visualization process that takes me through the nine servant leadership behaviors.

I mentioned this in an earlier chapter, so I'll just briefly go through my daily process here. I'm reminded to serve first when I make Lori's coffee in the mornings. When I pass the school bus stop on the way to work, it reminds me to build trust. Getting on the freeway helps me remember to live my values. When I get on my cell phone it represents the listening to understand behavior. The quiet time in the car reminds me to think about my thinking. The front door to my building at work is a reminder to add value to someone. Looking at my calendar is a reminder to be courageous. I think about someone that would like more of my time, so I can increase my influence. And then I think of a relationship that needs improvement, where I need to live my transformation. Those are all little deeds I live every day—little gateways, if you will—that remind me to live those behaviors. This process makes it real to me and easy to remember.

Long-Term Is the Goal

When we focus on being significant, we have to realize that our common purpose is not just about today, but the future as well. At Datron, we want to positively impact lives today *and* in the future. I love that part of the global defense company's vision that says, "We will define the future of defense." Your purpose has to be so impactful that it creates a burning desire in you and your people to devote your whole lives to it—not just a week or a month or a year. It has to be something bigger than you are and something that drives behavior at all levels.

During our transformation to servant leadership, I received a nice letter from Richard. Richard was one of the cofounders of the original Datron Systems, Inc. He was retiring from Datron when I joined them in 1997. I remember meeting him and our first discussion in Datron's new CEO's office as if it were yesterday. It was a typical corporate office, with the CEO as the center with a beautiful old solid wood desk, nice but somewhat outdated furniture—an area to receive guests and have those informal discussions. Richard asked me about my previous company and its CEO. After some discussion, Richard looked at me and said, "You must be a survivor." This was based on what he had heard about my previous CEO. I did not realize then that Richard would become such a supporter of Datron World after we purchased the company from Titan in 2004. As part of the purchase of Datron, we assumed his retirement agreement. We pay him a small fee for consulting that allowed him to stay active in our medical benefit program. We talk several times a year, and up until 2013, he would travel to Vista from Palm Springs once a year to have lunch with me. He provided me support (and prayers) for which I am eternally grateful. He wrote this letter on March 8th, 2006:

Dear Art,

I was blown away when I received your recent interoffice memorandum about Datron World's charitable fund. I had no idea the company had such a fund. Congratulations. I believe this is a marvelous thing. Although I'm sure there are many other companies, both public and private, that have such a fund too; I seriously doubt they contribute 10 percent of their operating income to it. Imagine, a company giving a tithe of its operating income to charity with 60 percent of it designated for ministry purposes. There is still some good in the corporate world; I just didn't realize how much of it was in Vista, California. Way to go!!!

On a more mundane level, I am also amazed at how well Datron World is doing since you bought it over fifteen months ago. Operating income in your first year of almost $6 million and over $3,700,000 in the quarter ended January 31, 2006. What kind of sales are you generating all this profit on? The US government order must have been huge. Are there other potential orders like this in the hopper? Congratulations again. You and your people are obviously doing a terrific job.

Do you share the financial results with your employees? I would be most interested in seeing any financial results and/or forecast you would be willing to share with me. I, of course would keep any information you give me strictly confidential.

Thanks again for all your human resource staff's kindness to me since you took over the company, particularly the free ride on Group Health Care cost you gave to the employees for significant portion of 2005. You are one generous guy. I am truly humbled by your actions.

Art, although, as I said, I am amazed, I couldn't be happier about the success you and your staff has made of Datron World. Keep it up.
Sincerely, Richard

Richard is still leading in retirement, thankful for Datron serving him while encouraging me to keep up the great work! Thank you Richard for living your life of service and paving the way ahead of me.

Are you a part of something that's bigger than you are? If so, are you living it every day and inspiring others to do the same?

PERSONAL

1. Do you live your company's purpose? Do you feel like you are a "part of something bigger?"
2. How do you give back to your community?
3. Do you want to be successful or do you want to be significant?
4. Create your own "elevator speech" that helps you visualize and live by the nine leadership behaviors.
5. What do you need to improve?

TEAM

1. How does your team inspire its people to live the company's purpose?
2. Is your team committed to investing in training for your people?
3. How does your team give back to your community?
4. Do you, as a team, seek to be successful or do you seek to be significant?
5. What does your team need to improve?

_____

_____

_____

_____

_____

_____

_____

Chapter Six Table Top Questions

7

Growing Leadership in Challenging Times

"…even darkness must pass. A new day will come, and
when the sun shines it'll shine out the clearer. Those were
the stories that stayed with you, that meant something even
if you were too small to understand why. But I think Mr.
Frodo, I do understand, I know now folk in those stories had
lots of chances of turning back, only they didn't. They kept
going because they were holding onto something."
—Samwell Gamgee, *Lord of the Rings*

"There are two types of businesses—those that have had
tough times and those that are going to have tough
times." So says Andrew Griffiths, who has written twelve best-
selling books on starting, managing, and growing small companies and is himself a serial entrepreneur. So the question for
servant leaders is not whether you will face tough times, but
rather how you will continue to grow your leaders and serve
your people during the tough times that will inevitably come.

Your Team's Maturing Transformation

Remember, when challenging times come, you will have
leaders at different stages of transformation. They're all
changing their beliefs and behaviors at different speeds, so
they're not all on the same page. Even in normal times, it's

difficult to manage those different transformation speeds and have your leaders come together as a team to get the results you need and serve your customers. In tough times it gets even harder. So before the tough times come, you need to understand and accept that challenge and be able to work with it.

For years I had managed people with different attitudes toward their work—some were straight eight-to-five people, never early and never late; some were always late; some always met their deadlines; and others always missed their deadlines. But even though I recognized the differences in people, I was still surprised when I realized the extreme differences in the speed of our team's transformation. Some were ready to cut their old mindset loose and move on. They had never been in an environment where they were exposed to the servant leadership way of thinking, but when they heard it, they believed it and were ready to go. Then there were others who just thought it was the latest and greatest fad of management, and they weren't ready to start that transition.

Since I was going through the transformation at the same time as my people and it was also new to me, I ran into several surprises along the way about how people transform. One surprise was that people will transform to a certain level and then stop; they won't go past that level no matter how much you try to help them. There could be multiple reasons for this, but here's how I look at it: As owners, we are devoted to our business because this is our life. This is what God has given us; it's what we're supposed to do. We will very rarely find people who will be at that same level of commitment with us. Many see their work as a career or a job, so they're only going to go so far. I understand that most people aren't willing to work as hard as an owner does, and that's okay.

My biggest surprise was the many different limiting beliefs that people have that impact their ability to transform their thinking into a servant-leader mindset. Most limiting beliefs come from past experiences. When we teach people to serve, some will latch onto that concept and say, "Yes, I'm supposed to help people, so I need to go find out what they need." Others will sit back and say, "I'll wait until they tell me what to they need." Those who sit back and wait have a difficult time moving forward in their transformation. Maybe they've learned from past life or work experiences, or a combination of both, that they need to take care of their own needs first, and they have a hard time getting past that limiting belief in how they should behave. I had some who believed wholeheartedly in servant leadership, but when it came down to the tough things—like mentoring people through their difficulties in transforming—they didn't want anything to do with it. Basically, they just wanted to teach servant leadership; they didn't want to do what was necessary to help people live it.

I had one leader who had a limiting belief when it came to confronting people. After trying to work with him for a while, I finally realized that he didn't understand our definition of confronting. His definition was the one that is standard in the workplace: I'm supposed to convince them that I'm right and they're wrong. In servant leadership, though, our job in confronting someone is to restore the relationship to what it once was. I call it my Biblical definition of confronting. Jesus never told people, "You're wrong and I'm right." He would create a relationship with them and then help them understand what needed to be done. This leader couldn't comprehend the difference, and that limiting belief wouldn't let him do what we were asking him to do. He finally sat down and said, "Art, if this is what you want me to do, I'm not your guy." He let his limiting belief stop his transformation instead of facing it and learning from it so he could move on. Some people will not go past that wall.

Limiting beliefs manifest themselves in many ways, and one is in fear. Some fear the environment around them, and others have different levels of fear of authority. For some, it's a fear of failure. At one point I discovered that some on my senior management team thought they always had to have an answer to any question that was asked. In fact, it had been deeply ingrained in them that it was more important to have an answer than it was to have the *right* answer. At times we would even have conversations that we knew weren't accurate because they were just trying to come up with an answer. It has taken a while to help them understand that it is okay to come into a meeting and say, "I don't know, but I'll find out for you," and then come back in a day or two with the right answer. In a servant-led organization where authenticity is valued, it's okay to say that to the boss. You won't lose your job because you don't know the answer on the spot. As leaders, we have to help them work through this limiting belief and fear of authority by mentoring them and standing with them rather than standing over them, and they are usually able to finally change this mindset.

There are some whose limiting belief is the fear of being judged if they say what they really think. They're afraid to say anything because they think someone will either say it's stupid or just brush them off and not let them into the conversation. That's usually because they've had that experience in the past when they've put an idea on the table. We teach leaders to judge others based on their potential and not their performance. We all have bad days when our performance—or our words—are not up to par. We want to capture that safe environment where people can talk about anything any time. At Datron we want to create an environment where our people can go to anyone at any time about anything and not be concerned about the organizational chart.

When I'm helping people get past their fear of being judged, I teach them to be aware of how they present themselves. For example, their tone and facial expressions have a huge impact on how their words are perceived and can send the wrong message if they're not careful. That's something I really have to watch, especially in my position as CEO. Sometimes I may not say a word, but the look on my face may come across as disapproval, when that's not really the message I want to send.

There are others whose limiting belief is the fear of rejection because they're not "smart enough." Maybe they don't have a college education or they've not earned a PhD, and they don't give their experience enough credit. I call it the "street smarts versus book smarts" conflict. I believe the best education is life itself. Education can certainly lay a good foundation, but its life experiences that really put that education to work. Some people think if they don't have an education, they don't have a right to speak up. I'll put "street smarts" right alongside "book smarts" anytime; I value both in my organization.

At some point people have to deal with their limiting beliefs in order to move forward. I keep going back to what Ken Blanchard asked me: "Do you really believe what you believe?" If people really believe what they believe about servant leadership, they have to move past whatever is limiting their transformation. Yes, past experiences can impact their ability to transform, but only if they let them. They need to remember what Coach John Wooden often said to his players: "Failure is not fatal, but failure to change might be." As leaders, our job is to help their transformations along by providing a safe environment for that change.

External Forces That Impact Your Business and Transformation

The speed of our leaders' transformation is at its highest level when things are going well in the company. People want to be part of that success and be on a winning team, and they are willing to change. But for various reasons, the speed of their transformation goes down during challenging times. Sometimes those challenging times are brought on by external forces over which we have no control.

Datron is an international business, so changing world events have a huge impact on our business. Our products are controlled by International Traffic in Arms Regulations (ITAR), which regulate the export and import of defense-related articles. Those controls affect our business on two levels—both the countries we ship to and specific organizations or people within those organizations. We could be denied access to an entire country, or we may be able to ship to a country but be restricted from shipping to a specific organization or individual within that country. Depending on events going on in the world, US officials determine whether they will support a country; and that can change on a month-to-month basis. So we may have been working on a program for two years, when all of a sudden the relationship between the US and that country starts getting cold. When that happens, the State Department could say, "We're not going to approve any transactions with that country." So we really have to be vigilant in watching international events that can affect our business.

Datron has a full-time compliance officer that keeps us in compliance with ITAR, as well as the US Foreign Corrupt Practices Act. Our international business is exposed to both politics and policies, not only in financial matters, but also in the human rights arena. The US is not in favor with most countries in the Middle East right now, so there will be times when those countries or organizations don't award jobs to American companies. That may not be the best way, but they let politics enter into their decisions.

Under the Foreign Corrupt Practices Act, a company or individual cannot give money to foreign officials in order to obtain or retain business. In our industry it's pretty easy to identify who the foreign officials are—like a country's Ministry of Defense or Ministry of Finance. But it gets a little tricky in certain industries, like the medical industry. In the US, representatives of the pharmaceutical companies can give out free samples to medical practices and hospitals. But in some countries the hospitals are owned by the government, which changes the picture. For example, a doctor in China who works in a state-owned hospital is considered a foreign official. So if a pharmaceutical representative gives that doctor free samples, this could be considered bribing a foreign official. But the most interesting illustration of this concept to me is Singapore

Airlines. It's a great airline; but since they're owned by the government, any pilot or flight attendant on the plane could be considered a foreign government official.

The strength of the US currency overseas impacts us, as well. When our dollar is strong, our customers buy less equipment, and when the dollar is weak, they're able to buy more equipment. With all of the regulations and international monetary issues in America, compliance with all the laws is such a challenge that small businesses are often prevented from even entering the marketplace. Even though we've been in the international business for thirty-five years and we have a level of competency that the normal start-up entrepreneur doesn't have, compliance is still an issue that impacts our business.

A big issue for us just within the last few years has been the attitude of officials in the US against defense companies. Some of them think we're just in business to get rich off of the government. Actually, they have no idea what it takes to run a business or the risks it involves. Business owners have to put up everything they own as collateral and guarantee that their businesses will perform, or the banks can take it all away. If you read defense articles, you will see that everyone is concerned about going into war, so they judge defense companies based on the fact that they sell products that are used in war. They don't understand that we provide freedom and security for countries. So they judge us based on what they think we are, and not on what we really are.

What Happens When Success Slows Down

When business is down, you're not meeting your goals, and business is shrinking, your core values will be challenged. You can't change your core values based on what the business is doing; you have to stick to what you believe and not change it just to get someone to give you an order. During these difficult times the servant leadership culture is really challenged. As people begin to second guess whether it works, you will start to see their behaviors—and maybe even their values—drift.

You have to stay more in tune with your people when that happens, but you can't change what you're doing just because times are challenging. You have to communicate more and make sure your people understand where the company is headed. You need to help them get through the tough times, while at the same time expecting them to continue serving others and not just doing tasks.

When times are challenging, people might say, "You know, I'm working really hard," and they think that replaces results. When one of my managers says that, my response is, "I agree that you're working harder in these tough times, but what results are we getting with that hard work? Are you working on the right things?" People often confuse action with results, and they aren't the same. You help them be strong through the tough times by giving them more support, because that's when old behaviors from their previous experiences come out. As the CEO, I have to have more grace when that happens and understand that that's when the power-leader tendencies are going to come out. And I have to watch my own attitude and behaviors during those times, as well. I have to have people around me who will say, "Art, you really blew it today in that meeting." Or, "Maybe you should think about what you said and go talk to that person; he's really feeling bad." You have to have people on your senior team who are willing to tell you that you messed up, and then you have to have the strength of character to listen to them.

In September 2009, the senior leadership team (my direct reports and I) went through a one-day meeting our own servant leadership behaviors. After listening for most of the day on how I was not meeting my staff's expectations of what a servant leader was, I couldn't remain silent any longer. My team expected me to be perfect in every way, in all my behaviors and all my communications. I had told them on several occasions their expectation wasn't realistic. I'm not perfect. I'm human and will make mistakes. When they finally asked me what I wanted from them I responded with "I would like you to extend the same amount of grace that I extend to you each and every day." I encouraged them to not hold over any ill feelings from day-to-day but start the day with a clean slate. I told them that is how I approach our relationship, extending grace anew each and every morning.

I received an email from one team member the next day that read "I confess that I am quick to point out the imperfections of others and slow to extend grace. Art, thank you for helping me see this during our SL training this week. Your point about extending grace anew each day was a very powerful learning moment for me."

Two months later, I really messed up in a business review meeting. I had called into the meeting late using a conference line, but had not identified myself properly. I was working from home after transitioning myself away from the weekly review meetings and turned the meeting over to them to run, so most of the time I was just listening. The next day I realized the team did not know I was on the call, a huge mistake on my part. It took me several weeks of reflection and listening to really understand how they felt about my behavior. I ended up sending the following message to my staff. "Based on my actions several weeks ago, the perception of the group is that I violated the trust we have between us. Perception or reality—it doesn't matter according to Matthew 5:23…if you have something against me, it is my responsibility to reconcile my actions and apologize. Please accept my apologies for violating our trust. I will commit to you that you will always be aware when I am present for a meeting or discussion. My hope is that you will forgive me and allow me to earn your trust back."

About fifteen minutes after hitting the send button on the email, one of my staff members replied, "Thanks to a lesson you taught me several weeks ago, I remembered to extend grace to you first thing this morning. I appreciate your apology and for role modeling an authentic journey toward servant leadership."

During the tough times, departments and groups have a tendency to move back into their silos. They want to protect their own teams. They're not sure what their future holds, and they want to make sure they have a future. Or those "little foxes" that are not in support of your servant leadership culture start to come out of the woodwork, and they start convincing other people not to be engaged. They spend more time *discussing* the future of the company than *doing something* to change the future of the company.

Sometimes when times get tough, we get wrapped up in the numbers. Leaders say things like, "We used to be a $200-million company, and now we're only at $100 million. We've failed!" In a servant leadership culture, we don't measure success in dollars; we measure success in influence. Some people tend to think, "The company's growing at $100 million a year; we should keep that up for a lifetime." Well, there are no companies that can keep that up for a lifetime. Everyone goes through tough times. And just because sales have gone down doesn't mean the company has failed; in our business it just means that we have a lot of outside events that have negatively impacted our business. If we allow the survival mode to kick in, we get into analysis paralysis, decisions don't get made, and everyone's power-model behaviors start to come back. And if you bring in new leaders from outside the company during these tough times, inevitably the people who have been around for a long period of time will stick together, and the people from outside the company will feel left out. Relationships that are already strong are the ones that bond together during tough times, and they don't let people from the outside in very easily.

Surprise Those Watching You and Your Organization

In tough times, people expect you to act like a company that's going through tough times. They expect you to let people go, close some of your operations, and stop helping people through charitable contributions and sponsorships. At Datron, we put a policy into place that ensures that every time we make a contribution to the fund, 10 percent of that money will be set aside for the future. We did that because we knew the business wouldn't always be on the upswing and there would be tough times, and we wanted to make sure there was money in the fund to help people during those times. We want to live our purpose at all times. That really surprises people in the community because they just expect our contributions to drop off the map when times are difficult. Our employees' attitudes stay positive, we have very little turnover, and we really enjoy helping people in the community during those times. People often ask, "How are you doing this?" and that opens up a whole conversation about our culture and beliefs. We don't compromise our values during those times; being able to continue helping people through contributions and sponsorships is important to us, and those things don't go away just because we're not the same size company we used to be.

It's interesting to discover during tough times who your supporters are on the outside—those who really believe in what you're doing. The minute those tough times arrive, some of your supporters will disappear, because they prefer to be associated with the "successful" companies with high revenue and profits, rather than "successful" companies that value influence more than profits.

In December 2015, a pipe broke near our building in Carlsbad, California and flooded our entire first floor. That happened on a Friday, and we had lined up a crew to come in on Saturday and dig down to identify where the pipe was broken. We wanted to get it fixed as quickly as possible. In California we have an entity called "Dig Alert" that coordinates that kind of dig with all the utility companies to make sure you don't hit an underground cable or pipe. The contractor we were using told us, "We can't contact Dig Alert until Monday." That would not only have delayed our work; it would have also left us without fire protection, as the fire protection system was shut down.

I placed a call to a city official on Saturday morning and I explained our situation to him and told him we needed his help to get through the red tape. He said, "Art, give me a couple of minutes and I'll call you back." Five minutes later I got a call from the city manager. He said, "My Department of Water Works is on it. Someone will be calling you soon." Ten minutes later I got a call from the department head, saying, "I've asked one of our staff to go get all of the information you need to bring the utility companies in. We'll take care of that for you." He asked if I would be on site, and I said, "Yes, I'll be right here." An hour and a half later, they arrived on site and he said, "I've called all the utilities, and they're going to be out sometime today." By nine o'clock that night we had clearance from all four utilities, and we started digging the next morning, Sunday.

As we were feeling encouraged by all of the help we were receiving from our city officials, we remembered something that happened two years before. A fire had burned the offices of a company up the street from us. We had some empty space in our building and I called the mayor and asked him to let the company know we had space available in our building. Then a real estate broker contacted us and said, "We'll need to prepare a lease." I said, "No, I'm not going to charge you. I have space and you need space. Come and use it for free." I said, "I'll help you get up and running on the internet and anything else you need." The fire was on Friday, and they were up and running on Monday. The mayor wanted to recognize us, and I said, "We're just doing what we're supposed to do. We don't want any awards or recognition." So when we needed help, the mayor took care of us. When you go through tough times, you'll find out who your real friends are; they are the ones who will jump in and help you. Thank you to the mayor of the City of Carlsbad and his staff.

Some Will Not Make the Journey

One thing you have to understand, especially during tough times, is that burnout is real. People sometimes try so hard to transform that they will burn themselves out. As leaders, we need to watch for little changes in attitude and behavior, and then stick close to people who are struggling and not just assume they're okay.

I learned this lesson the hard way. I had one leader who had been with this company for many years. He had a lot of things going on in his life, and at the same time there were a lot of things happening at the company. In fact, it was during a time I was in the hospital. He burned himself out trying to do everything. He had been completely on board with servant leadership, so we didn't stay close to him and didn't realize he was struggling. We thought he was okay. We missed that one. When we look back, we realize we should have been sensitive to the things we knew were going on in his life. When times get tough, the possibility of burnout increases; people are trying to overcome obstacles to get results while trying to transform their behavior at the same time, and that can be overwhelming for some.

When you go through tough times, it's important to learn from them and put systems and procedures in place that will serve as a safeguard in the future. Last year we came up with a way to really focus on what the expectations are and get people on the same page. We call it GRP—Goals, Roles, and Process. Now when we're dealing with a tough situation, we say, "What's our goal? What's the role of each person in the room? And what's the process we're going to use to address that problem?" When everyone is on the same page and working together, you help draw that fear down.

We invest a lot of money in training. For example, we've taken our leaders to Hawaii several times to create experiences that would help them transform. The danger we get into when we see someone who isn't as strong as we thought they were is to think, *I made that investment and it didn't do any good.* That's a trap that CEOs have to avoid, because investment in people is always good; it's never bad. One thing I've learned over the years is to make the investment but manage the expectations from that investment. In other words, be careful not to have expectations that the investment is going to take you somewhere you really don't have a chance to be; manage your expectations based on the investment you've made. Then, just like when you invest in a car or a home, you have to take care of it. You have to continually make investments to keep it looking nice so you can maintain the value of the investment. The same applies to people; keep investing in them!

When they go through tough times, some companies show their misguided priorities. They might say, "I can't afford any training time," or they might do counterproductive things like making their people use tools longer. They stop investing in their people. They reduce their benefits, and then all they look at is their productivity. They don't understand that in order to keep a workforce engaged and productive, you need to invest in good benefits, like a good retirement plan and a good education program. And yet that's often the first thing to go when times get tough.

But sometimes, even when you continue to invest in your people during the tough times, there are some who won't make the journey with you. That's when you have to make tough decisions. I recently heard Alan Mulally speak; he's the former CEO of Boeing who went to Ford Motor Company and had a tremendous impact on turning the company around. When he went to Ford, he implemented some of the things he had done at Boeing. And when people would come to him and tell him they were having a tough time changing their behavior, he would tell them, "That's okay." Someone might come to him and say, "I'm having a difficult time making this change," or, "I'm having a difficult time thinking the way you want us to think." His response would always be, "That's okay." He said, "You know, about the fourth or fifth time you say '*That's okay*' to someone, they're going to ask, 'Well, why do we need to change anything then?' And his response at that point is, 'That's okay. If you don't want to change to help the company get better, then I'll have to move you to some other role within the company or help you find a role in another company, but that's okay.'" That was a great way for him to create a sense of security for his people. He was communicating to them that just because they can't change their behavior at Ford, it didn't mean they were bad people. He assured them, "It's okay. I'll help you find a place where you'll be okay."

I have one last piece of advice for when people you've cared about and invested so much in don't make it: Show grace, but don't be naïve. By that I mean, stay close to those your gut feeling tells you won't make the journey with you, because you don't want to keep them around too long. You don't want to be naïve in thinking they're going to transform at some point in the future, and then end up letting them stay and continue creating havoc in the organization because they're not on board with the program. The damage they can do is much greater. Remember, though, they're not bad people. They just continue to have limiting beliefs—which usually come from past experiences—that keep them from transforming. Show grace, but don't be naïve.

Onboarding of New Leaders

When you bring on new leaders all the time, you will need to onboard those new leaders. Some will be promoted from inside the company and some will come from the outside. Remember, the job of the CEO is to put the company's leadership puzzle together. I love the puzzle analogy, because there are times when you think a piece fits and it doesn't, and then later you find out that there's another piece that fits better. That's how it is when you bring in new leaders. You think they will fit in a certain area, so you put that puzzle piece together with another leader of the company. Then after a while you realize the fit is not right, so you take it out and go find the right puzzle piece that it fits with. You're continually putting a leadership puzzle together so people can help each other and learn from each other. You're constantly looking at pieces to make sure they fit with the right pieces.

Leaders who come in from outside the company bring their experiences with them, and of course those who come from inside the company bring their internal experiences. In your onboarding process, figure out a way to get the internal and external leaders to respect each other's experiences. How do you get the people who have been together inside the company for fifteen years to respect the knowledge and experience of the person you just brought in? The danger is that you may have people pitted against each other simply because they don't trust each other. Our job is to build that trust. Their combined knowledge is most beneficial when it works together.

I've learned that when you bring in new leaders to your servant leadership culture, it's important to stay close to them. There's a saying in one of Ken Blanchard's videos: "It's easier to loosen up than to tighten up." What that means is, don't loosen up with new leaders right up front. Stay close to them, and then loosen up as they earn your trust in their ability to make decisions in accordance with your values and culture. Don't give them free range to make all the decisions up front, only to realize later that you have to pull them in.

When you have someone leading your company, you need to make sure you know their heart. You can test their skills, and you can test their character to some extent; but finding out what's really in their heart is tough. We've grown up in a society where people feel that it's important to be seen in the right light. They feel that how other people see them on the outside is more important than what is on the inside. And unfortunately, they really are often judged by how they dress, what type of car they drive, and the house they live in. Consequently, people put on masks and don't let others see their true character, so you have to closely watch their behavior and see how they handle certain situations. Part of our training for new leaders is to give them a mentor who is outside their department. We believe it's important to have a mentor who will "talk turkey" with them without the threat of having their authority standing over them.

And it's important to hold your senior leaders to a higher standard. You expect more of them. I love what the Bible says about teachers. It says if you're a teacher of the Word, then you're going to be held to a greater level of responsibility and expectations. The same thing goes for senior leaders who teach others in the organization—we are all held to a higher standard.

What to Do When Leaders Are on the Sideline

You will have some leaders who let their fears dictate their behavior, and they won't participate. They don't want to get involved in conversations to help find solutions. They're happy just being a manager and they'll say, "Just tell me what my job description is, and I'll do that. I don't want to be involved in finding solutions and making decisions."

For some roles in the company, that's okay. In Datron's Compliance Department, for example, you want to have people with a legalistic mind. It's always nice if they also have a heart, but it's their legalistic side that keeps you out of trouble. But you can't have people in manufacturing sitting on the sidelines and not being involved in finding solutions to make the process better, especially if they're in a leadership position. They don't have a choice; they have to be involved. Most of the time when you have leaders who don't want to participate it boils down to their self-worth and fear. They might wish they could contribute, but they don't believe anyone will listen to them if they did or what they say doesn't have value.

And then you have those who have a hard time implementing a command decision that a leader has made. A command decision is one that a leader makes when he doesn't have agreement within the team. Servant leaders don't enjoy making command decisions that go against input from some on their team, but sometimes there's no way around them. When that happens, the expectation is that once the decision is made, the team will fully support the decision. Young emerging leaders, especially, seem to have a hard time with that because they're being asked to respect the authority they've been placed under. In our culture, we've been trained to challenge leaders if we think there's a better way, but sometimes that involves respecting their authority when they make a hard decision.

I really appreciate John Maxwell for helping me understand that concept. He said, "When you disagree with a leader but you're still able to implement the decision he or she has made, then your character is right and God can give you more." How you react to authority is a reflection of your character, and your character has to be right before you can be given more responsibility. I know I wouldn't be doing what I'm doing today if I hadn't adjusted my attitude about authority. And that applies to any relationship.

Culture is Fragile

We have dedicated our lives to servant leadership and have spent many years implementing it. I was very surprised, then, to find how easy it was for the leadership team at Datron to drift away from its commitment to this practice. It was slight and it was subtle, but there was a drift. When I hired a new CEO and he brought in other new leaders, the onboarding process was not what it should have been. In reality, this culture or mission drift happens in all companies, but that doesn't mean it has to be permanent. We will go into this in detail in the next chapter when we talk about sustainability, but I recommend that you read a great book called *Mission Drift* by Peter Greer and Chris Horst that will help you fully understand this concept.

Mourning That Comes with Reductions

There will be times when you have to make adjustments in tough times, and sometimes you're left no choice but to implement a reduction in work force. There's an old saying associated with that: "It's just as tough on the leaders as it is on those it affects." That's a cop-out and a bunch of hogwash! A reduction in workforce is not about the leader. You're impacting people's lives and shaking their entire foundation! You have to understand that and be respectful of it.

At Datron we've had some tough times when we knew we had to do a reduction in workforce near the end of the year, but we made the decision to keep people on through Christmas. We decided not to do it during the November/December time frame, and we didn't care about the impact our decision would have on our cash flow.

And we are sensitive about medical coverage for our people, because that's one of their biggest concerns. A lot of companies will do a reduction in workforce at the end of the month; but we always do it in the first week of the next month, because that gives our people another month of coverage. The experience is unpleasant enough, and we want to make it as easy as possible for the employee as we can.

We've also changed the way we handle our reduction in workforce process; we've found a better way to be sensitive to people's feelings. One of the biggest things we realized that caused that change is this: The day before the reduction, we trusted everyone. Why should that change on the day we have to take the action? Like most other leaders who were brought up in the power model world, I was taught that when you have a reduction in workforce, you can't trust the people anymore. So you have to escort them to their office, watch them pack up their belongings, take them off work duty so they won't have an opportunity to sabotage their computer, and make sure they exit the building within the shortest time possible. There's no chance for any adjustment or mourning. But I will be forever grateful for a judge who once challenged me on that process. He said, "You're a servant-led organization, right?" I said, "Yes." Then he said, "Then why did you only allow twenty minutes from the time you told the employee you were letting him go to the time you walked him out the door? Twenty minutes! You didn't give him any time to adjust." You know, he was right. I came back and said, "We're going to change our process."

The next time we had a reduction in workforce we did it in the morning, and we told people, "You can stay around all day long and you can finish your work shift. You can go talk to the people that you've been hanging out with at work. You can do whatever you want to for the whole day—get on your computer, send emails out to people, finish any projects you need to transition to someone else—whatever is best for you." And we had a major positive reaction to that, both from the people who were impacted and from the people who remained in the company; they saw we treated people with dignity and respect.

There's a time for mourning. You and your leaders will go through the ramp-up to make the decision, and then you'll go through the event. Then you need to allow time to just sit with people and give them a chance to talk and be sad. It's a cycle you go through. It's more than just getting through the day, and then once the day is over, it's over. We've had several people say, "I want to come back to work; so when things pick up, call me." There have been times when we've been able to bring people back, and we get excited and celebrate when that happens. It's a good thing!

Reductions in workforce impact everyone, including the leaders. I think one of the times it impacted me the most was when we decided to sell our printed circuit-board assembly line and outsource that process. The last ten people who worked on the line were all hard-working people, and I had to call them into a conference room and say, "We have to end your job." I apologized to them for having to do it. I took it pretty hard because those people were losing their livelihoods. I excused myself and went into a nearby conference room to gather my emotions. And four people walked into the room behind me— four people who were losing their jobs that day—and they all hugged me and said, "Art, it's going to be okay." They were telling me it would be okay, and they had just lost their jobs! That's the kind of transformation you see in people when you invest in them and care about them—they care back. And that's priceless for a servant leader.

PERSONAL

1. How far are you willing to go in your transformation to servant leadership?
2. Do you have any limited beliefs that affect your ability to transform?
3. During tough times, do you stick to the servant leadership behaviors and the company values?
4. When you disagree with a leader, can you still implement his or her decision?
5. What do you need to improve?

TEAM

1. As a team, are you totally committed to transforming to a servant-led organization?
2. How does your team help your people get past their limiting beliefs?
3. During tough times, does your team stick to the servant leadership behaviors and the company values, and do you help your people do the same?
4. Evaluate your team's process for reduction in staff. Are people treated with dignity and respect?
5. What does your team need to improve?

_____

_____

_____

_____

_____

_____

_____

Chapter Seven Table Top Questions

8

Sustainability: Key Principle to Your Long-Term Success

Mission True organizations know why they exist
and protect their core at all costs. They remain faithful to
what they believe God has entrusted them to do. They
define what is immutable: their values and purposes, their
DNA, their heart and soul…To remain Mission True is to
adapt and grow, so long as that adaptation and growth does
not alter the core identity.

—Peter Greer and Chris Horst, authors of *Mission Drift*

In an interview for a blog, Ken Wytsma asked Peter Greer, coauthor of the book *Mission Drift*, "What are some of the major warning signs of mission drift?" At least four of the ten warning signs he listed stood out like neon signs to me. They were all signs we had missed at Datron, and they've now become part of our story.[9]

And that's the part of our story we want to tell in this chapter. We've told the fun part—how we bought Datron World Communications, changed it to a servant-led organization, and grew it into a very successful company that has impacted the lives of many people. It is a great success story, and people love to hear that part. But mission drift happens—

9 Ken Wytsma, a blog, "Peter Greer on Mission Drift,"
http://kenwytsma.com/2014/04/15/peter-greer-on-mission-drift/ (accessed 12/27/15).

sometimes when you least expect it—and we are compelled to tell that part of our story as well. We want to help you recognize the warning signs and avoid the pitfalls that lead to culture shift.

Culture Is Fragile

When I brought in the new leader (CEO) in the spring of 2013, I thought the servant leadership culture at Datron was pretty solid. We had implemented servant leadership eight years earlier, and I believed it was ingrained into our organization. We had a leadership team that was active in all of the servant leader behaviors, and since I thought it would be better if there was only one leader in the building, I decided to relocate my office to our Palomar facility, which is about five miles away. I believed our culture was strong enough to hold true, so I let him run with it.

The new leader had a good heart, and all the signs pointed to his commitment to transform from power-model behavior to servant-leadership behavior. I made some assumptions that our company culture was strong enough that the management team could help him with his transformation, and I was meeting with him monthly. During the first eight months, everything seemed to be going okay. The business was struggling a little, but I saw no indications that there were any real challenges. There were some major changes in the US defense budget that impacted us, but we thought we could deal with that.

The new leader hired some people he had worked with in the past; and even though I knew there was some risk in hiring people from a large, corporate, power-model environment, I believed our culture was strong enough to help them adjust to servant leadership. We had training and systems in place to accomplish this, as well as a team dedicated to the servant leadership culture. What I somehow missed was that his belief in the power model was greater than his desire to transform his behavior to a servant leader. So without my daily presence, he went to where he was comfortable: the power model. And that's what people do—go where they're comfortable.

By the end of 2013 I wasn't feeling well, but I thought I was okay; I found out in January I wasn't. I went into the hospital in January of 2014 for thirty days and didn't come back to work until June, so I was out for about six months. I encouraged the team at Datron to help the new leader learn about servant leadership, and I believed that's what they were doing.

When I entered the hospital, Lori became very protective of me and kept people away. And she didn't give them a lot of information about what was going on—it was a while before she even knew herself. So the people at Datron lived in the question mark for about two months. They weren't sure what was going on, and I think there was some talk that I may not even make it back. With the absence of information, people usually assume the worst.

I started to get better and was released from the hospital at the end of February. During the month of March, Lori and I met several times with the new leader at our home. The business was still struggling, so we decided we had to do a reduction in workforce. We had a serious disagreement with the new leader about the best way to go about that; and for some reason, I didn't put two and two together and realize at that point that his belief in servant leadership was not as strong as his belief in the power model. That was the moment, though, that I started to realize that something wasn't right.

When I came back to work full-time at the end of June 2014, I discovered that our servant leadership training program for new employees had basically been put on hold. There had been talk of doing some training, but it was going to be a very small portion of what we normally did. And there was no emphasis on holding the leadership accountable to the servant-leadership behaviors. The new leader had created his own inner circle of people—including some who had been at Datron for a while. We literally watched about three or four people move away from servant leadership and go back to the power model, and it seemed like it happened overnight. Lori and I thought, *Wait a minute! We've invested eight years of training. We've poured our hearts into these people. Why is it so easy for them to go back to their old ways?*

That's when we started to realize that the culture of the company had really changed, and it had happened quickly. The new leader's influence in the company probably started to take hold about four or five months after he came on board; so the culture shift happened within a matter of about eleven months, from late summer of 2013 to the middle of 2014. When I got sick, his influence just took off because he didn't have any oversight. I believe he thought the company was in danger, and he just went back to where he felt the most comfortable; that was a natural reaction. I would later find out how strong his belief in the power model was.

Mission Drift

I didn't know anything about mission drift until I heard Peter Greer speak at a leadership conference. He talked about organizations that had started out with Christian values, like Harvard University and the YMCA, and how quickly they moved away from those values once the founder or the driver of those values left the organization. I read the book later and thought it was pretty interesting, so I started looking around at my organization. That's when I realized that I had made a big mistake in moving out of the building when the new leader came on board. The mission drift had started when I wasn't around to keep my voice strong with the leaders. Even though our values had not changed and our mission and purpose had not changed, we started drifting away from them both.

In September 2014, I discovered a bombshell. Each quarter we donate 10 percent of our operating profits to our charitable fund, and that has never been up for discussion. That has always been the first thing we did after the quarter ended. I came back in June 2014, and in September I discovered that the contribution to the charitable fund for the 2013 year-end had never been made—a contribution of $675,000. When I realized that, I said, "This has gone way too far." That charitable fund represents the very core of our purpose—it's our main avenue for helping people. I was devastated to realize that my senior staff had bought into this decision, and none of them ever brought it up with me. When I started asking about that, they all said basically the same thing: "I now report to the new leader, and I have to follow what he says."

Authority and Its Deep Roots

At that point I began to realize how difficult the authority issue is for people. The new leader wanted to use the cash for other things, and none of the senior staff felt any accountability to stick to our core values and do what we had set up to do— what they knew was not up for discussion to change. When I came back, I met with him once a month to review what he was working on and his priorities, and he always came across as someone who really cared about servant leadership. But he wasn't being transparent about who he was, and I bought into it. The entire time, from when I hired him in the spring of 2013 to the time I came back in June of 2014, I really thought I had a handle on things.

I call the kind of authority he had "passive power" because he wasn't demanding at all. He didn't raise his voice at people; he was very nice. A lot of people liked him. In fact, I liked him. But he influenced people with his power in an indirect way. As I looked back at all of this, I realized how fragile the culture really was. And I had to ask myself, "Why did it go that way?" I understand that people, including myself, have been taught that you don't buck authority. And then add to that the natural reaction of protecting yourself and going into survival mode when there is conflict. I think that's what happened to the culture at Datron. The staff went into survival mode, even as they were pulling back.

I believe the culture shift started when the company did not donate the money into the charitable fund. Then they started to pull back on the training. In the past, we had always found the money for training. I would have even written a personal check for it if the company hadn't been able to pay for it. That's how important it was to me. What it really came down to was the priority the new leader put on servant leadership was much lower than the priority I put on it. And the culture around him wasn't strong enough to curtail the backward pull because he was the person in authority.

When I had a discussion with some of my staff after I returned about helping me get servant leadership back in its rightful place, I learned that part of the problem was that some didn't want to confront people. In our servant leadership behaviors, we confront people from a Biblical standpoint, where the goal is to restore the relationship to what it once was, not to convince the person that you're right and he or she is wrong. However, I discovered that some of my senior staff had never latched onto that definition of confronting, and they operated under the world's definition of confronting—that they had to basically beat people up to do what I wanted them to do. So at that point, I had to make some tough decisions, and that was the most heartbreaking thing I went through in that whole process of turning the company culture around.

Are Your Leaders Strong Enough to Survive Without You?

It's interesting to see how past behaviors stick with people. You may think, *Our culture is strong. We're doing a lot of training, and everyone is following the right behaviors.* I've discovered that when times are good, it's easy to keep the culture in place. But when the company starts to struggle and new leadership is brought in, there's a tendency to change everything you've done. Those old files start to click in, and people start to go back to old behaviors. I was astonished to see how quickly the work we had done for eight years got turned around.

A couple of months after I came back to work in June of

2014, I received a letter from our bank calling a loan we had with them. As it turned out, our account had been transferred from the San Diego branch of the bank to the Los Angeles branch. We had a great relationship with the commercial lending branch in San Diego where my staff provided information on an as-needed basis. The banking branch in Los Angeles didn't take the same approach and required that we meet all the terms and conditions of our agreement. Our staff did not adjust accordingly, which resulted in the bank calling our loan. My assistant and I worked for an entire day getting all the information together, and within twenty-four hours the bank had a package with everything they needed. After that incident, the bank didn't want to do business with us anymore, and that caused some major problems for us.

As a result of the conflict surrounding that issue, a member of my senior staff resigned and I had to step back in to fill his role. When I started dealing with the bank, it led to further accountability and transparency issues. I finally had to say it was time to move on. I had to put the culture back together, and it was not going to happen under the new leader's direction.

When I built my team, I thought that team would be in place for a lifetime. Unfortunately, I lost most of my senior staff in the aftermath of turning the culture back around. When I look back, though, I realize how many people within the company were strong enough to say during that time. Their attitude was, "This is going to pass. I'm going to stay here." I lost very few managers during that time, although I basically now have a brand new senior staff. That's because I started with the senior staff and held them accountable for what was going on in the company. I didn't go down into the organization and say, "You're done and you're done." I went to the senior staff and said, "I hold you accountable for the culture here." I had some tough discussions with them.

You have to figure out a way to hold people accountable to the culture—especially your leadership team. You have to make sure they keep your core values and purpose in place when they're making decisions, and you have to ensure that your culture is sustainable for the long term.

Some of the key people who helped me get servant leadership started here at Datron are gone today because they didn't keep servant leadership as a core behavior in my absence in 2014. That puzzled me because we hadn't just gone through the motions; we had some great transformations. In spite of our best efforts, culture shift had happened because I was not aware of the danger signs.

You don't just hold people accountable to make money. Making money is the easier part. The question is *how* are we going to make that money? I think about what Datron went through in that year. We had a horrible year in 2014 from a financial perspective, and anyone looking at the financial records would think we really failed. Yet we look at success in how many people we influenced that year with servant leadership and how many people we helped with the charitable fund. That fund didn't go to zero because we lost money; we were good stewards of what God had given us, and we put it to use in the right way and in the right time. It's not just about giving money away. We believe being good stewards includes doing it in the right time frame. We were able to continue our work with the charitable fund even though we were going through really tough times financially and our culture was struggling to survive.

Danger Signs—What to Watch For

I spent time thinking about my thinking for a year—thinking about what went wrong and wondering what I could have done differently. I kept coming back to the conclusion that culture is really fragile. You can't assume, as I did, that your culture is strong. You always have to keep communication going. You have to keep putting your purpose in front of people and showing them how to impact others. Your leaders have to maintain their servant leadership behaviors. It's not just a matter of training your people to go through the steps and then moving on because you think everyone is doing well. You really have to stay on top of the culture. In my situation, I had to look myself in the mirror and say, *I didn't hold myself accountable. I wasn't transparent enough. I contributed to the mission drift we experienced. I didn't serve my senior staff very well.*

It's been said that it takes five years to see the effects of leadership training and seven years to change an existing culture. We made it through those first seven years, but then the question became, "You've changed the culture; now how are you going to sustain it?" And sustaining it becomes even more difficult when you face challenging times. Authority really plays a big part in that. The presence of authority freezes some people; they can't make decisions because of their fear of disapproval or their fear of failure. Most of the time, they're not reacting to the person in authority; they're reacting to the experiences they've had in life with authority. And that's part of the culture shift that happens; when times get tough, people go back to what they're comfortable with. In survival mode they go back into their shell, and they won't go out on that limb and take risks for fear of losing their job. You have to recognize where they are and help people through that.

I'm coming to the realization that you're very fortunate if you get 50 percent of your people to jump on board and get transformed to the point that the transformation sticks. We can all change for a little while. I just have to look at my struggle with weight to understand that. I can go work out for a long time and lose twenty or thirty pounds. Then I think I have it beat and I slow down my efforts. I don't continue working out with the same stringent regimen, and before I know it, I've put the weight back on. And then I wonder what happened. I've been through that cycle way too many times in my lifetime.

When I meet with other CEOs, my peers, I hear stories about successful companies whose businesses have slowed down. What we've learned is that when times are great and things are going well, we as leaders become complacent. We feel good about the way things are going, and we think life is easy. We agreed that if we had it to do over, there were things we would do differently, including watching for the danger signs in culture shifting.

One of the major danger signs is a change in the behavior of some of your key leaders—when they let things slip that are important to you. Our key purpose required we put money into the charitable fund, and that went by the wayside in tough times. I came back in and said, "That's not up for discussion. When we make money, we contribute. Period." Unfortunately I discovered this after the fact, but that was a huge indicator for me that our culture had shifted. I knew their excuses were only a cover for the shift—"We were so busy we forgot," or "We didn't have enough money so we allocated what we could and we're going to do that when we have more money."

Another danger sign is that your team's work performance starts to slip, and your department groups start to go back into their silos. They retreat into their safe zones and start trying to solve problems by themselves instead of putting them on the table so everyone can help. You might see a management team that worked really well together start going into silos under new leadership because that's the way the new leader operates. I saw the new leader create a divisive senior team and management team, and as the leadership goes, so goes the organization.

It may take a while for people to get used to going back to the right behaviors. I can't change their mindset or their behaviors overnight. I can only change myself by being a better leader through behaviors. I can talk all I want to, but I'm not going to gain their respect back until I perform and get results through the right behavior.

Another thing to watch out for is those who support the individual and not the company's purpose. They are the ones who have the potential to fall first because their support is tied to the individual and not to the position. When the leader leaves, the position is still there and they need to support and respect the person who fills that position. But if their support is tied to the individual instead of the position, they're going to go the way of that individual. That mindset is so prevalent in our country. How many times do we hear people talk about our president by his last name without putting "president" in front of it? He's the president. Call him president. I like the way they handled that in the TV show *West Wing*. It didn't matter whether the president agreed with them or whether they had a great conversation or a tough conversation with him; when the conversation was over, they always said, "Thank you, Mr. President." Always respect the office. I am often asked what my advice to those in government is. Simply put, I believe we need to serve the people and not the ideology. Serve people first! Treat everyone with dignity and respect. Learn from our mistakes and build a bridge of love, not hate. Visualize our country where everyone comes together in love for each other for the sake of people, not ideological platforms.

Accountability, Transparency, and No More Excuses or Victims

People love to be victims of their circumstances, and some people aren't strong enough to change how they feel about being a victim. It doesn't matter how hard you try, you're just not going to be able to change them.

When I challenged one of my staff members about the things that had happened, she had a little bit of a victim attitude. She couldn't find her new identity under the new leader, and when we held her accountable for her actions, she wanted to push it off and say, "It wasn't my fault." So I worked with her for about two months to help her find another job. She asked if I would serve as a reference for her, so I had a nice conversation with the president of the company she was interviewing with, and she got the job. Our job as servant leaders extends past the current situation. We help others succeed, even when it's not within the four walls of our company.

Turnaround or Accept

When I stepped back in as the leader, I had two choices: I could either accept what was going on if I was not strong enough to turn it back, or I could turn the situation around. I had every excuse in the book not to get back in and fight for the culture. And, honestly, there have been times when I've thought, *I don't know if I'm strong enough to do this again.* But I just keep reminding myself that I play to an audience of one (God), and He's the only one I need to please. Living my purpose each day will bring more joy in my life.

We finished 2015, and we made money for the year—quite the turnaround from 2014. We had a decent backlog, so we had another good year in 2016. Our turnaround was gaining steam and the servant leadership culture was beginning to thrive once again. Financially, we made a dramatic turnaround from our dismal 2014. In 2017, the year we just finished, we had great sales and profits, re-establishing our historical levels while entering into a record contract for the company valued at $495 million. This year, 2018, looks to be a banner year for the company, and we couldn't be happier for the Datron team.

We're in the process of updating our leadership training based on everything we've learned since we developed the training program, and we started implementing that the following summer. We brought Stephen M. R. Covey in to help us with trust, because that was broken after I stepped back in. So we're investing in people and bringing in help from the outside, and we're making good progress.

I basically have a new senior staff. My CFO, who has been with me for several years, is a wonderful young lady who has a real desire to take care of business. She's still learning how I look at things and sometimes wonders why I'm not worried about cash flow at certain times. I just tell her, "It will come. It will be okay." She represents the company and servant leadership extremely well to the community. Two of the men on my senior staff were elevated from the management team, so they were home grown. I just promoted a manager who's been with us for a long time to the position of VP of Sales. I didn't have to rebuild my entire team; I had people who were ready to step in.

One of the things I had to learn in this whole turnaround situation was that I needed to live my servant leadership transformation with everyone—not just the people I got along with or those I worked well with. There are people here who supported the new leader and what he did; they believed in him, and now they're being asked to believe in me again. I know that transformation in their belief will take some time, and I can help them along by living my transformation with them and treating them just like I treat everyone else. When you want to be seen as a partner by people in your organization, you have to act like you want to be a partner. You can't sit back and expect people to come to you just because they report to you. So living my transformation as a servant leader with everyone in the organization, regardless of whether we're on board with each other or not, is my challenge. That's what will help turn it around.

Because of my illness I could have decided I was not strong enough to do this again. I could have accepted things the way they were and just tried to make as much money as I could, and be happy with that, not caring about our culture. I get tired, just like the next person; and when that happens I want to be by myself and not talk to anyone. But that man in the glass came out, and I had to decide what kind of person I wanted to be. Did I want to help turn it around again or accept it the way it was? I decided I could not see our organization not live its purpose in positively impacting the lives of others today and in the future.

PERSONAL

1. Do you see yourself staying true to the culture of your company, even during tough times?
2. Think about what your role would be if and when you start to encounter culture drift.
3. If your new authority figure did not fully embrace servant leadership, would you feel obligated to follow his or her lead?
4. What do you need to improve?

TEAM

1. How strong do you think the culture of your team is? How strong is the culture of your company?
2. How should you as a team handle any culture drift when you first encounter it?
3. Discuss a possible plan you could put in place to prevent culture drift, especially if a new authority figure did not fully embrace servant leadership.
4. Are your onboarding procedures strong on commitment to servant leadership?
5. What does your team need to improve?

_____

_____

_____

_____

_____

_____

_____

Chapter Eight Table Top Questions

9

Ultimate Measure of Servant Leaders

"Life's most urgent question is,
'What are you doing for others?'"
—Martin Luther King, Jr.

You may be wondering, *What does all this mean for me? How can I tell whether my leadership is making a difference?*

I think you will agree with the above quote by Martin Luther King, Jr., that we all have a calling to serve people. You wouldn't be reading this book if you didn't, no matter what your religious affiliation is or whether you choose to have one at all. And if you're going to devote your life to serving others, you naturally want to know that you're making a difference. So I want to end this book by showing you how to go about measuring the difference your servant leadership is making.

Key Performance Indicators

When we finished our first two levels of servant leadership training at Datron, we brought an education consultant in to evaluate how well we did. In the process of setting up a survey that would help us do that, they told us that it takes an average of five years to really see the effects of leadership training, and it takes eight years to change a culture in a company whose culture is already established.

When prospective clients ask, "What's the return on investment for the training you're proposing?" we tell them, "There is no return-on-investment formula for you to calculate." Their next question is, "Then what key performance indicators do we need to set up to track the effectiveness of the training?" Early on, we started recommending that our clients track engagement and trust—especially trust. Trust is the biggest key performance indicator that tells you how effective your training has been, and we have a very simple survey that we use to measure it. Most of our clients think our survey is too simple, though, so their human resources department usually takes over the survey process. They end up with a survey that's longer than it needs to be and it becomes a burden for their employees. Having a lengthy survey also makes it difficult to glean results. They go overboard in the process and then have to choose one or two things from the survey to focus on to help them be successful in turning their culture around.

We recommend setting up a trust index by asking only two questions of everyone in the organization: 1) Do you trust your boss? 2) Do you trust management? Then we recommend that you ask your management team an additional question: Do you trust each other? We suggest that companies run this survey at least twice a year, and in some cases once a quarter, so they can get regular feedback on the trust issue. As mentioned earlier, the trust survey results over the years are included in the appendix.

Beyond that, we usually suggest that companies select one or two of the key performance indicators they are already using, and expect those results to get better. That way they can track the performance indicators that management is already seeing, rather than setting up something new. The end goal is to see improvement in the results of the business. It would be useless for us to go in and measure something the company is not already measuring and show them improvement in that area but not show them any improvement in their results. Our clients can see a lot of merit in that approach.

Most companies have their own surveys to measure employee engagement. There are a lot of engagement survey instruments in the marketplace that you can subscribe to. We don't recommend any particular one because we want the companies to evaluate the surveys and determine what works best for them. In those companies that do an annual survey, we encourage the department heads or group managers within those companies to take one to three items they know are important to management and ask those questions in their own group survey every three to six months, making it a sub-set of what the company does on an annual basis. They can use Survey Monkey or any other survey technology that's easy to use. Some companies don't allow outside survey software on their network for security purposes, but most of them will have some type of simple survey software available.

One of the other simple surveys we do every month, using Survey Monkey, is asking our management team to tell us how much of their time, on a percentage basis, they spent investing in their employees that month. We just want them to estimate how much time they spent in one-on-one time with their people. Our goal is 20 percent, but we encourage them to be honest, no matter how much time it was. Then we use that information in their self-reflection process—*not* in their evaluation process. As CEO, I have the same goal of investing 20 percent of my time with the people who report to me, and it's in those mentoring relationships that we focus on self-reflection. In most of the organizations we work with that are having challenges, we find that the leaders aren't investing enough time with their people. There is a direct connection, and that usually includes the breakdown in trust.

The top line is: there's no need to create something new, other than creating a trust index if you're not already doing that. Pick one or two performance indicators you're already tracking and set a goal for improvement in those areas over the next six to twelve months. After you see the results of the surveys, set up initiatives to improve in those areas that show weakness.

Once you start surveying, it's important to share the

results with everyone who participated in the survey, rather than keeping the results to yourself. When outside companies ask us to participate in surveys—usually dealing with salaries, incentives, or engagement—they encourage our participation by promising to provide us with the results of that survey. If people invest their time to take a survey, they usually want to see the results. So we encourage you not to keep the information to yourself, and don't filter the results by deciding what's important to share and what's not important. If you ask ten questions, share the results for ten questions.

By selecting performance indicators you're already tracking, taking surveys of those indicators on a regular basis (quarterly or every six months) and then sharing that information with everyone who took it, you can achieve increased employee ownership in performance.

Before we move on, I would like to ask you the purpose of the surveys you take in your company. Take a moment and make a short list of your expectations. Now rank your expectations in order of importance. Surveys are used for so many reasons in today's business world. I suggest the most important reason leaders should conduct surveys is to provide a basis to engage in conversations with your employees. Engage in direct, human conversation with those you ask to take the survey on how you and your organization can improve.

Do Those You Serve Grow?

Robert Greenleaf, who is considered the founder of the modern servant-leadership movement, suggests the test for servant leadership is: "Do those served grow as persons? Do they, *while being served*, become healthier, wiser, freer, more autonomous, more likely themselves to become servants? *And*, what is the effect on the least privileged in society? Will they benefit or at least not be further deprived?" I believe that in order to answer the question, "Do those you serve grow?" you first have to find out where people are. You have to get to know them and find out what their gifts are, what they love doing, and what they don't like doing. Then you can help them grow in the areas where they want to grow.

There are any number of ways you can help people, depending on what their individual needs are and where they want to go. That might involve putting them in a different position to utilize their gifts. It might be supporting them in their educational goals, and that could be more than just paying their tuition. We had one staff member at Datron enroll in an executive MBA program that was done mostly online, but sometimes required attendance at classes in a different state. They were not required to take personal time off; we paid her during those times she had to be away during the week. Others may need encouragement and hope in dealing with the challenges of life. Just make sure you are invited into that area before you offer your help.

Sometimes when people leave our company voluntarily, especially those in our Engineering Department, it has nothing to do with money; they want to be more challenged technologically or some other way, and we want to support them by giving them an opportunity to grow at another company. "Do the people you serve grow?" doesn't come with a requirement that they stay employed at your company. Corporate America has a difficult time dealing with this one, because most of the time when they invest in people, they want them to stay. Servant leaders don't look at it that way. Our concern is whether the person grows; and if that means letting them go to a better opportunity, we let them go. We know we've impacted that life to the extent we can, so we let them go somewhere else and enjoy that. We all like to see our companies grow, as well, but we have to see that we grow in the right way. We ask ourselves, "Does it matter how we grow, or is it just about growth?"

Here's our challenge to companies that really want to practice servant leadership and help their people grow: Time is the most valuable commodity you have. Give it to your employees; let them see that you're investing your time in them. And that doesn't mean just going down the hallway and saying,

"Hi, how are you doing?" It means putting your direct-reports on your calendar and investing thirty to sixty minutes in them on a regular basis. Our proven theory is that, if the leaders invest time in their employees and help them grow, companies will see great improvements in the annual evaluation process they already have in place. As Theodore Roosevelt once said, "People don't care how much you know until they know how much you care." The best way you can show them you care is to take the steps to meet them where they are, and that involves investing your time in them.

"Do those you serve grow?" is a very relevant question in servant leadership, and it doesn't have a time frame on it. People will grow at different speeds. They will grow faster in the areas they're comfortable with, and their growth will be slower in the areas where they're not comfortable. You have to understand that process and be patient. I keep what I call a "cheat sheet," which is a list of notes I keep electronically on everyone that I meet with one-on-one. After each meeting I record the things we talked about or the challenges that person had on that date. That way I can keep better track of each person's growth. I can compare where they are today with where they were, say, a year ago. Maybe I needed to spend an hour with that person a year ago talking about issues, and now I only need to spend fifteen minutes. You'll find that as people grow, both their trust in you and their confidence in themselves increase, and they are able to make more decisions without your input. There is nothing more rewarding than seeing people latch onto something, learn about it, understand it, apply it in their life, and then hear the stories of how that impacted their life. I think the true measure of servant leadership is the life stories that come out of those we serve.

Succession Planning: Who Takes the Helm From You?

As you know from previous chapters, I've had some front-line experience with choosing the wrong person to take the helm from me. Even though the person I hired as the new leader passed all the gates in the interview process, I missed some of the signs along the way. I learned a lot through that situation, and I want to share what I've learned with you.

I cringe when I hear someone say, "We need a succession plan." When I ask them what it means to have a succession plan, they usually say, "The organization needs to know who's going to take over our company or our department. We need to put a name there so we can develop that person." I keep going back to the fact that, on average, we're going to have our emerging leaders in our companies anywhere from two to three years. How do you prepare a succession plan when your emerging leaders will be changing jobs that often? I think succession planning is being redefined by the world we live in, especially by the emerging leaders who are searching for something that has purpose. When they don't find it, they have no problem going somewhere else. So if you don't have a purpose in your organization that people can really latch on to, you can't have a succession plan; you're going to lose the people you want to pass the company or department on to.

The emerging leaders require purpose in their lives, and they want to find someone who will develop them and help them live that purpose. But they don't want to get in line. One of the reasons I left Disney when I did was because I could only get promoted if the person above me got promoted, retired, or passed away. Since Disney was a great company and people loved to work there until they retired, you had to wait in line; and I decided I didn't want to do that. That was over thirty-five years ago, and even back then I wanted something different. Two of the leaders at the company I went to work for after Disney taught me the value of building products in manufacturing, and I found my passion there. I've been building things ever since.

I think it is so important to pick the right person for every job. I was with a group of CEOs a while back, and we were talking about someone who was a great technical asset for the company, but his character wasn't a match. I made the comment,

"We're too hesitant to make decisions based on character; we'd rather make the decision based on competence." When we look at new leaders at Datron, we look at their character first and competence second. We can train on competence a lot easier than we can train on character. A select few companies can successfully hire based on competence first, but only because their brand has already filtered character before people even apply. Most companies don't have that kind of brand recognition.

Once you hire the right person, you have to develop that person and make sure he or she is latched on to the purpose of the company. And it's not just a matter of saying it; you have to see the person living it through his or her behaviors. What "living it" means to me versus what it means to you or someone else may be two different things. I can say I live it twenty-four-seven because I've invested in the company and told the bank if I don't perform they can take everything I own. I've put everything on the line, and I'm willing to take that risk. Other people will say, "I will live the purpose of the company, but I'm not going that far. I'm not willing to put up my home." And of course I don't expect everyone to do that, but I hope we can find some who would say, "I believe in this so much that I'm willing to give it my all, and that includes everything I own." I realize that those people are few and far between, but often the person who takes the helm will be required to live the purpose to that extent.

When we went through the hiring process with the new CEO, I spent over ten hours talking to him, and he passed all the gates. I had such a high level of confidence in him, with his industry background and his heart to serve, that I think I was lulled to sleep. I didn't think I needed to stay next to him to help him understand why we did the things we did and make sure he was running the company the way I would. If I had it to do over, I would have kept my office next to his for six to twelve months. What happened was totally unexpected because we had checked both his character and his competence.

Here's what I think I missed: I saw someone who wanted

to serve people, but the power model had been ingrained in him for so long that he reverted back to where he was comfortable when he ran into some pushback on servant leadership. And because I was not in the building to see it, I wasn't there to help him through it.

My process will be different when I pick someone to run the company when it's time for me to leave. Succession planning plays into seeing that the company continues with its purpose of helping people. So I will develop someone who is already in place (or will be at that time)—a person who has clearly and substantially proved his or her commitment to our purpose.

Are Others Better Off After Coming in Contact with You?

I think this is where the real nature of servant leadership lies, because we can have such a tremendous impact with the small touches we make with people in the community just by our actions and the things we say, even if we are only in contact with them for five minutes. We want people to feel better about themselves after they come in contact with us. Sometimes we do that by giving them money, but at other times there may not be anything of worth exchanged. There are many other ways we can help people—with a smile, a pat on the back, a word of encouragement, a thumbs up, or even just eye contact. We may never see that life again, so we need to think about how we will impact that person in the few minutes we've been given.

Servant leaders need to maintain a continual thought process when it comes to serving people. We can't just serve those who are in the box that we're comfortable with. We serve those put in front of us, even if we disagree with what they believe. Every person counts. So we have to continually be thinking, "How am I going to influence this life? How am I going to serve this person?"

Joyce Myers, a well-known Bible teacher who has her own television show, has been known to get onto people who go to the marketplace and leave their grocery carts by their cars instead of putting them in the rack in the parking lot. I've heard stories about people who were putting their cart in the rack at the same time someone else was, and they both just looked at each other and said, "Joyce Myers, right?" Just that little act of putting the grocery cart in the rack where it belongs is the result of someone being influenced by listening to Joyce Myers. You can have that same kind of influence on people in your life; and once they start doing something positive, they will impact other people.

I think there's more power here than there is in the "Do those you serve grow?" metric. I think the words, "Do those you serve grow?" applies to those you're investing time in, consciously and intentionally. But this metric, "Are others better off after coming in contact with you?" applies to those you just come in contact with, and it's usually unintentional on your part. I really believe this is a bigger measure of servant leadership.

There's a program here in San Diego County through a non-profit called the Alpha Project that helps men who have had problems with addiction and/or crime get their lives back together. Once they enter into this program, they have to go out into the community and earn money to put into their own bank account, and they have to have a certain amount of money in their account before they can go on to the next level of the program.

At one time, a local newspaper company used to donate newspapers to this organization, and the men would go out on the street corners and sell the papers on Friday, Saturday, and Sunday. They were called "hawkers" because they were hawking the papers. All the money they collected from selling the papers went into their individual bank accounts. Since these men were trying to put their lives back together, I encouraged people to not just dig in their pockets for a quarter when they drove up to get a paper, but to give them the first thing their hand touched in their pockets, whether it was a five-dollar bill, a ten-dollar bill, or a twenty-dollar bill. They're driving a car, so they could certainly afford it! I would tell them to roll down their windows and say, "Hi, how are you doing?" and ask the man's name and how he was doing in the program. The man might look at them kind of funny, and they should say, "No, really, how are you doing in the program?" He might say, "Pretty good," and they should say, "Here's some money." When he says, "Here's your change," they should say, "No, put that money in your bank account." Then they might add something like, "You know, that light at the end of the tunnel on the road you're on is a lot better than where you came from. Keep going with the program." That takes maybe fifteen or twenty seconds to influence a person's life while they're sitting at a red light. I've seen men fly as high as a kite for two to three weeks after someone rolls down their window and says "Hi" to them, and then gives them a ten-dollar bill for a twenty-five-cent paper so they can put it into their bank account. It means so much to them that someone cares and wants to be part of helping them get back on their feet.

I tell this story everywhere I go, and now I have people in the community thinking, *When I see these men, I want to help them. I may not necessarily want a paper, but I want to help this life.* I think that's why this is so powerful. We can tell the stories of people trying to turn their lives around, and it makes people want to be part of that story, even if it's for fifteen seconds. They may never see that man again, or they may see him again next week on the same corner, but they have that fifteen seconds to make an impact.

There are programs like that all over the place where people are trying to get their lives back together, and we can do little things to help them that we normally wouldn't even think about. It's usually spontaneous and unintentional. Wouldn't it be great if everyone would participate in helping others less fortunate than themselves?

We have another program here in San Diego County where the firemen go out into the community a couple of times a year and stand on the street corners to collect money for burn victims. It's called a boot drive, and they actually use a fireman's boot for people to drop money into. There are fire trucks on the corners and the firemen are running all over the place collecting money. It's great to see people participate in this like it was a community event. Everyone wants to help.

Giving Back by Living Your Purpose

I want to throw out a challenge here to corporate leaders: Give back to the communities your corporations do business in. Make helping people in your marketplace a part of your purpose. Most companies' purpose is to be the greatest this or the greatest that, or to be the most trusted supplier of this or that. The community you do business in, the community where you get your employees from and that provides your services, is a big part of that purpose, whatever it is. Corporations have a responsibility to give back to those communities. And it isn't just a matter of giving back in the form of hiring a lobbyist to impact legislation or backing a political party or politician. I'm talking about giving your money to a charitable organization that's making a difference in people's lives, giving back to the educational institutions, investing in people's education, helping to get the homeless people off the streets, or helping people get their families together. Whatever it is, you have a responsibility to give back to the community that helped you generate the profits for your stakeholders.

The Soft Results: Human Kindness and Happiness

The CEO of a large survey company recently told someone I know that, based on many of the surveys they do, they've discovered that citizens in the US are very lonely. We can look around us and see people who are not engaged at work and people who are struggling with their lives. These people may or may not have a belief system, but they are people who have just had some hard knocks in life.

I just did a tweet recently that I think fits here: "Embrace the mystery of servant leadership. Serving first creates amazing results and brings purpose to your life." Having purpose in your life brings happiness. Having happiness in your life brings kindness that you can extend to others.

That's the soft side of servant leadership. You're creating a community of people who are living life to its fullest, and that brings joy to everyone, even in the tough times. I think the difference between servant leaders and other leaders is that servant leaders see hope when others don't. I think servant leaders sing when there's no music, because they're playing to a higher purpose. Sometimes I forget that I'm really called to serve an audience of one, and that's who matters. When I remember that, I believe my positive influence on people's lives multiply.

Servant leadership brings out stories of people overcoming challenges; and I think when people share their experiences about coming through those challenges, they realize they now have the ability to help others get through those same challenges. People hear their stories, and their hope is stirred to believe that they, too, can overcome.

As we come to the close of the Datron Servant Leadership story, I have several notes I've received to share with you. The first is from Stephen M. R. Covey. I met Steven's father at a leadership conference where I heard about *The Speed of Trust* for the first time. I immediately was fascinated by the idea that trust in an organization could either be a tax or a dividend (for those that haven't read the book, buy it and read it to find out). I wanted a copy of the presentation but was unable to get a copy so I had to read the book. I would later meet Stephen M. R. Covey when we asked him to teach our leadership team about *The Speed of Trust*. He accepted and came to Hawaii for one of our leadership off-site meetings. We learned so much from Stephen; I love working with him, love his heart to teach and serve others. After the time in Hawaii, I received the following hand written card from him.

Art, I just wanted to let you know what an amazing experience I had with you and the Datron team in Hawaii. You are a great model of servant leadership and the results you are achieving brings credibility to the approach. I commend you for this. I hope you found our Speed Of Trust work to be valuable. I look forward to reconnecting with you and your team. With admiration, Stephen.

The other note I would like to share is from Mark Sopp. I first met Mark Sopp when Titan bought Datron Systems, the parent company to Datron World Communications. He was the CFO of Titan Corporation. I worked closely with his staff during the due diligence process prior to closing the sale of Datron Systems with Titan. Mark was instrumental in helping me purchase Datron in 2004. I remember speaking to Mark after we closed the purchase of Datron from Titan. He told me not to waste this opportunity. I always remembered his advice and appreciated his help in securing Datron World. Several years later Mark would leave Titan and become the CFO at SAIC. I saw Mark at a local Chamber event called Meet the Leaders that the Vista Chamber holds each year. Datron has been an active supporter of the event. After I sent Mark a quick note, he responded with a hand written note sent by US mail (yes, some of us still do this):

Thank you for your note. Again it was a delight to see you and John at Issa's event, and also at the Century Club from afar earlier in the year. I remain in awe of what you and the team have accomplished at Datron. It is a great story and example of entrepreneurial and leadership success! I'd love to come by and visit in the April to June time frame; I'll give you a call! Best – Mark S.

Very special notes from two different perspectives in life, that influenced me through my own servant leadership journey.

My final story is about an organization that builds wheelchairs for disabled people around the world call Free Wheelchair Mission. I became aware of this organization when one of Datron's employees submitted a grant request. Below are some photos of the people they helped in Ethiopia. The note that came along with the photo's read:

> Thank you so much for Datron's contribution to the Free Wheelchair Mission. It is hard for me to describe what an impact that will make. When I was in Ethiopia in November, I saw people dragging themselves along the ground or being carried from 25 kilometers away by their entire village. One man said that he had been to the district headquarters five times before because he heard there would be wheelchairs, only to find out it was untrue. He left with his first wheelchair. God bless all of Datron. – Bill.

You can tell in the photos that the wheelchairs are made from plastic chairs you and I might have on our patio. The founder of the organization puts wheels on them with support bars and sends them to foreign countries where the need is the greatest.

I would later hear about the child of a parent who was unable to walk. His daughter was so excited about her father getting a wheelchair that she dressed up in some traditional celebration clothes. For the first time in her life she would be able to sit in her daddy's lap after he had received his free wheelchair.

Positively impacting the lives of others today and in the future. I love our purpose and the stories we get to be part of. How are you using what God has given you? What are you doing with your leadership gifts, your serving heart to impact the lives of others?

Start the journey; you will not regret it. On the journey with you always. For the sake of others, with dignity, respect, and love.

—Art Barter

PERSONAL

1. Do you trust your boss? Do you trust management?
2. What difference(s) do you see in your life since you started the transformation to servant leadership?
3. Do those you serve grow?
4. Are others better off after coming in contact with you?
5. Have you seen that living your purpose helps you bring kindness to others?
6. If servant leadership has made a difference in your life, have you shared your story with others?
7. What do you still need to improve?

TEAM

1. How has the trust indicator for your team changed since you've implemented servant leadership?
2. What key performance indicators are you watching to gauge the effect of servant leadership on your team? Have you seen an improvement?
3. Do those your team serves grow?
4. Does your team hire for competence or character?
5. How does your team give back to the community you do business in?
6. Share with each other your story of transformation or the stories of those you serve.
7. What does your team still need to improve?

Chapter Nine Table Top Questions

Epilogue

Your Legacy as a Leader

I think all leaders go through a time when they question what type of leader they are. Actually, that is part of the process in transforming to a servant leader, and you don't get that answer overnight. Until I met Ken Blanchard in 2003, I thought I was on the path to becoming a great leader. But Ken challenged my thinking one night, both as a leader and as a believer, and I've been on a different path ever since.

When you're faced with life-changing challenges, I believe you have to be ready for them before you will take action. In today's fast-paced world, we're bombarded with information and challenges from many different directions, but we only respond to what we're ready to receive. If you're ready to start thinking about the type of leader you are now versus the type of leader you want to become, you have to decide where you want to go with that and the legacy you want to leave behind.

I'm a little uncomfortable with the word "legacy" because I'm not doing servant leadership to build a name for myself. I want to influence people and help them understand how to help other people, and that's the most important thing for me. I only want to be known as that person who cares about people and helps them realize their need to be a different kind of leader. The transformation won't happen until they do. If "legacy" is the right word for that, then so be it.

We started the Servant Leadership Institute because we

wanted to get the conversation started. We wanted to light the fire and spread it everywhere we could in order to get people talking about it and moving on to implementing it. We knew that once we got the fire started, it would quickly spread to the point that it would be out of our hands. And it has done just that; it's taken on a life of its own. There are flames of servant leadership burning in Africa, as well as Europe and Asia because of our efforts, and we certainly support that but we don't have to be there to keep it going. The wildfire spreads when we bring like-minded people together in our conferences every year and give them an opportunity to tell their stories of transformation, which illustrate the difference servant leadership is making in people's lives. I think about that time when we laid people off and four of the women followed me into the conference room to tell me it was going to be okay. That's the type of difference we want to make in people—when in tough times they can tell even those who are taking something away from them, "It's going to be okay."

On the flip side of that, we've always said that we only want to work with people who are ready to grab this and run with it. I'm not here to debate people; I'm here to help them.

The World Needs to Change

I think you can just look at the newspaper headlines over the last year to realize how badly the world needs to change. What many people don't understand is that we need to change what we're doing in order for the world to change. The freedom we experience in America comes with a responsibility to treat everyone with dignity and respect, even those people we don't agree with. We need to be able to disagree with people without anger. (I'm not talking about foreign policy and the issues of war, here; I'm talking about Americans getting along with each other.)

I use a phrase in workplace violence training that we all need to remember: "Anger is one letter away from danger." The anger that is happening in this country today is really one letter away from a catastrophe. We're seeing it more and more. What kind of nation are we leaving for the generations following behind us?

Challenge to Be a Game Changer

As leaders, we need to change that game. Leaders can't get into arguments and yelling matches. They need to be the calm-headed game changers in the world who say, "We can all get along; we just have to figure out how to treat each other with dignity and respect."

I keep coming back to dignity and respect, because right now that's what is missing in this country; and that lack of respect is bringing our country down. What kind of nation are we creating for our kids and grandkids? We have to be the game changers, each in our own part of the world. We have to be able to step up and be courageous in our communities and in our companies and demand the right kind of character in all the organizations we're responsible for. Yes, I said "demand." We have no choice but to demand that everyone in our organizations respect each other. It's no longer an option. It takes courage to be that kind of game changer—the same type of courage it took for our founding fathers to risk everything in order to create a nation free from tyranny; the same type of courage it took for Dr. Martin Luther, King, Jr. to rally people together for the unpopular cause of bringing about civil rights in this country; and the same type of courage it took for Todd Beamer to say in the face of death, "Let's roll."

Servant leadership is a game changer, and I think it is really starting to take hold. But people are starting to attach different names to it, like "authentic leadership." I think we need to call it servant leadership because the word "servant" implies action. The action required in servant leadership is the act of being intentional in helping and serving others, and bringing a positive mindset to the world. It's imperative that we put the word "servant" in front of the kind of leadership we need for this country right now.

For the Sake of Others

I have to constantly remind myself that I'm doing this for the sake of others, not for myself. Wherever humans are involved, the ego is always present. I like what Ken Blanchard says: "Ego really stands for 'Edging God Out.'" I think we have to continually ask ourselves as leaders, "Are we doing this for ourselves or for the sake of others?" Sometimes I want to say to some of our political and community leaders, "Wake up!" With the unrest we have in the world today, imagine the change that could happen if everyone in our government and in our communities acted on good intentions for the sake of others.

For me, personally, servant leadership is the only way to go, and I hope after reading this book you agree. Serving others first is the only way to create a future where everyone can coexist in peace and accomplish together what we can only dream about as individuals. I see it as the answer to many of the problems we see in the world today. I invite you to join me in being a game changer.

Living Life to the Fullest

When I spend time reflecting about our journey in servant leadership that started in 2003 with Ken and in 2004 when we purchased Datron, I wonder what my life would have been like if I was taught servant leadership in school—if Management 101 was about serving others instead of me. The journey of Datron by year, from 2004–2018, is presented in summary form in the appendix. This summary shows our journey based on the roadmap presented in this book. We hope this helps you create your own roadmap in servant leadership. The world today needs servant leadership now more than ever. What would our communities, our nation, and the world be like if we treated each other with dignity and respect? What if we serve people instead of an ideology? What if we lived our lives for the sake of others? I think that is my definition of living life to the fullest! What's yours?

Appendix

DATRON WORLD COMMUNICATIONS, INC.
SERVANT LEADERSHIP JOURNEY

ROAD MAP

FISCAL YEARS
2004 2005 2006 2007 2008 2009 2010 2011 2012 2013 2014 2015 2016 2017 2018

1 Create and Communicate
Who Are You, and What Do You Stand For?
Live What You Stand For
Communicate to Inspire Your Organization
Champion Your Organization's Purpose
Behaviors and Language of Servant Leaders

2 Educate to Own
Spreading the Word
Add Value to Your Leaders through Education
Investing Your Time for the Good of the Organization
Understanding How to Live Your Education
Small Groups
Creating Team Memories

3 Empower Ownership: Not What You Think
Ownership Defined
Leadership Team Ownership
Transferring Ownership to Your Leaders
A Challenge: the CEO's Desire to Control
Patience and Discernment
Getting Out of the Way
When Leaders Don't Grasp the Empowerment Being Offered
Listen to Understand

4 Measure Transformation and Results
Creating a Safe Environment for Failure
Small Groups
Geese and Leadership
Measuring the Transformation of Leaders
Managing the Different Speeds of Your Team's Transformation
Businesses Must Create Results
Educate, Understand, Apply, and Reflect

5 Reflection - Business Reviews of a Different Nature
Key Reflection Traits
Monthly Management Team Investments
Quarter Management Team Off-sites
Investing Money Into Developing Your Team
Keeping Yourself Healthy

ROAD MAP	FISCAL YEARS
	2004 2005 2006 2007 2008 2009 2010 2011 2012 2013 2014 2015 2016 2017 2018

6 Living Your Purpose Day to Day
How Will Your Organization Live the Common Purpose
Put Your Money Where Your Mouth Is
The Stories Will Come When You Live Your Purpose
Success versus Significance
Long-Term Is the Goal

7 Growing Leadership In Challenging Times
Your Team's Maturing Transformation
External Forces That Impact Your Business and Transformation
What Happens When Success Slows Down
Surprise Those Watching You and Your Organization
Some Will Not Make the Journey
Onboarding of New Leaders
What to Do When Leaders Are on the Sideline
Culture is Fragile
Mourning That Comes with Reductions

8 Sustainability: Key Principle to Your Long-Term Success
Culture is Fragile
Mission Drift
Authority and Its Deep Roots
Are Your Leaders Strong Enough to Survive Without You?
Danger Signs - What to Watch for
Accountability, Transparency, and No More Excuses or Victims
Turnaround or Accept

9 Ultimate Measure of Servant Leaders
Key Performance Indicators
Do Those You Serve Grow?
Succession Planning: Who Takes the Helm From You?
Are Others Better Off After Coming in Contact with You?
Giving Back by Living Your Purpose
The Soft Results: Human Kindness and Happiness

10 Your Legacy as a Leader
The World Needs to Change
Challenge to Be a Game Changer
For the Sake of Others
Living Life to the Fullest

LEGEND: ▫ Survival Mode ⌐ ┐ Learning & developing mode ■ Implementation mode ■ Getting it mode

Trust Index

We were introduced to Stephen M. R. Covey's the Speed of Trust in 2007. We learned from Stephen's trust work the following two questions are the best overall indicators of the health of an organization:

1. Do you trust your boss?
2. Do you trust management?

Datron began asking those questions several times per year in a very simple setting—our quarterly All Hands meetings. Next to each of the questions above, we put Y/N and asked our employees to circle Y for yes or N for no. The charts below show our results. During our recent fiscal year 2017, we obtained our highest yes percentage.

2017 Trust Index	% of employees indicating "yes"
Do you trust your boss?	90%
Do you trust management?	84%

We started surveying our employees in 2007. The results were as follows:

2007 Trust Index	% of employees indicating "yes"
Do you trust your boss?	77%
Do you trust management?	57%

We've experienced a 17 percent increase in trust with our boss and an amazing 47 percent increase in trust with the management team.

We added one more question to our trust index beginning in 2008. We asked our leadership team (any employee with a "Manager" or higher title).

3. Do you trust each other?

Our first survey result on this question was at 50 percent. Our most recent survey in early 2017 was 100 percent; a 100 percent increase in trust within the organization's leaders!

Start a trust survey TODAY with your organization and get serious about building trust.

Datron World Communications Trust Index FY 2007 - 2017			
	Trust Boss	Trust Management	Trust in Leadership
2017	90	84	100
2016*	80	75	85
2015*	80	60	50
2014*	80	75	75
2013	82	78	96
2012	85	73	85
2011	85	73	85
2010	72	63	85
2009	75	63	73
2008	80	60	50
2007	77	57	N/A

denotes estimate by Art Barter, CEO

Datron World Communications Trust Index Comparison FY 2007 - 2017			
	Trust Boss	Trust Management	Trust in Leadership
2007*	77	57	50
2017	90	84	100
% increase	17%	47%	100%
Δ 2016 to 2017	13%	16%	30%

denotes estimate by Art Barter, CEO

One-on-One Meeting Time Survey

We asked our leaders to spend at least 20 percent of their time each month meeting with the people in their organizations. Each month, we sent a simple survey question via SurveyMonkey.com. We asked them to estimate how much of their time was spent that month in one-on-one meetings. They simply had to tell us an estimate (like 12 percent). We didn't ask them to keep records, check their calendars, or report any details of their meetings. We simply wanted to know the percentage. Each month, we would report one percentage for the entire leadership group: a simple average from those that responded.

We kept it simple, easy, and focused on changing our behaviors. We never published the results in a chart. We instead encouraged our leaders to spend time discussing our values and servant leadership behaviors. We set out to create that safe environment of investing time in others, creating relationships that would change the DNA of Datron.

Journaling

I was never a fan of journaling. I never understood the value in recording my thoughts or challenges, or even my successes. That all changed when I was facing a difficult decision in my life.

Before making my decision, I decided to get away by myself—away from all the free advice from friends and family. So, I left on a trip, driving up the coast of California for one week.

During the week, I decided to stop at several locations a day, quiet spots where I could take in the beauty of the coast and think about my thinking. I decided to record my thoughts, questions, and revelations about my life so far. I learned to ask myself questions like: *What did I do to create this situation? "Where do I want to go? How do I know I am making the correct decision?* Over time I would pull out the journal and read it. That process of looking back helped me realize how much I'd grown as an individual and as a leader. I learned a lot about myself that week.

I continue to journal today. It has become an important part of my life, of how I learn about myself, and challenge myself to get better. It is my hope that when I die, my journals become a source of wisdom for my children, Jennifer and Chris.

As a gift to you at the end of the appendix, I have enclosed the introduction and first chapter from my book *The Servant Leadership Journal: An 18 Week Journey to Transform You and Your Organization*". Enjoy! Start journaling today!

Datron Servant Leadership Training

We created a training program at Datron to teach all of our employees about servant leadership. The training program was forty-five hours in total, divided into three modules of fifteen hours each. We developed the first two modules and trained everyone from this material. Prior to developing the third module, we hired an educational consulting company to help us evaluate our training. A survey was given to our employees to provide insight on where the training was successful and what we should consider in developing our third and final training module. The following is the evaluation report prepared and presented to the senior staff at Datron after the survey was taken.

Evaluation Overview

In January 2010, Datron World Communications, Inc. engaged an educational consulting company to design and implement an evaluation of Datron's Servant Leadership Training Program.[10] The evaluation assesses participant learning and understanding of core concepts, participants' perception of the relevance and usefulness of the training in relation to their work at Datron, participants' ratings of the level of their own servant leadership qualities, and the perceived sense of organizational support for servant leadership challenges and implementation.

While servant leadership is used by many companies (i.e. Starbucks, Google, and Southwest Airlines), the challenge to credible, empirical research on the effects of servant leadership is incorporated into various organizations. The training and implementation varies widely from company to company. A majority of companies using servant leadership train only their upper management or their customer service personnel. In the case of Datron's approach, *all* employees are trained in

---

10 The selected consultant had no previous experience or relationship with Datron, Servant Leadership Institute, or any partners that developed the training program.

servant leadership—from the on-the-line assemblers to senior staff members.

Second, and a much more problematic issue, is that of how to assess servant leadership training and its impact. Measuring servant leadership is quite difficult as it is most often only defined as emphasizing the leader's role as steward or the resources in the organization and encourages leaders to serve others while staying focused on achieving results in line with the organization's values and integrity.

Stakeholders, or those with vested interests in the findings of this evaluation, certainly include Datron's management and the Servant Leadership Institute. In addition, sharing the evaluation findings with all staff may go a long way in reinforcing the value of the training and engaging all employees in the process. Externally, other companies interested in or engaging in servant leadership might find this study helpful for planning and implementing their own programs. While this study is not a rigorous, random experimental design, it has the potential for creating a more-than-anecdotal account of the achievements and challenges in servant leadership.

Evaluation Questions

The approach used for this evaluation is that of utilization-focused evaluation or, more simply, an evaluation focused on investigating the effect of a program by presenting credible relevant data to stakeholders for the purpose of continuing program improvement. The overarching evaluation questions for this evaluation were:

1. What did participants learn?
2. What did participants think about what they learned?
3. What do the answers to questions 1 and 2 mean for the next level of training?

The evaluation sub-questions listed below articulate the focus of these overarching evaluation questions.

- How well did participants understand the concept of servant leadership *after* and *prior to* the training?

- How well did participants understand how Datron's mission and purpose are aligned with servant leadership *after* and *prior to* the training?

- How well did participants understand the interpersonal skills identified *after* and *prior to* the training?

- How did participants rate their own servant leadership qualities *after* the training?

- How useful or relevant to their work and lives was the training to participants?

- Did participants report any significant issues related to challenges or concerns about servant leadership in general or their role in servant leadership?

- How did participants rate organizational support available for implementing what they learned in the training?

- Given the findings related to each of the sub-questions above, what implications do the findings have for level 3 training and/or Datron's servant leadership training overall?

- For all sub-questions above, did analyses broken down by employee groups reveal any significant differences in participant responses to survey questions?

Evaluation Methods

Utilization-focused evaluation is based on the premise that evaluations should be judged by their utility and actual use. Use is defined as how real people in the real world apply evaluation findings. The methods used in this evaluation are focused on obtaining the information both most valuable and relevant to stakeholders and the most useful to them for understanding the effect of the program to date on employee understanding of servant leadership, what the learning meant to the participants, and where the program goes from here.

For this project, the data collected are primarily qualitative in nature. That is, there are no test scores of numerically scored rankings. The survey designed included both multiple-choice and open-ended items. Some items had "Agree to Disagree" type response categories and other items had choice options with qualitatively defined, or criterion ranked choices. This type of qualitative or criterion defined levels provides clearer levels of participant understanding of various concepts presented in the training. On the following page is an example of this type of qualitative response question:

How would you rate your understanding of "effective listening skills" AFTER your servant leadership training?

- I don't understand what effective listening skills are.
- I have a little understanding of what effective listening skills are.
- I have some understanding of what effective listening skills are, but I'm not confident in my understanding of how to apply them in my relationships.
- I have a good understanding of what effective listening skills are and how to apply them in my work at Datron and in my relationships.

Data for the project were collected using an online survey. The education consultant assigned Datron employees random ID numbers produced from a random number table. ID numbers were not sequential nor were they assigned in any particular order. ID numbers, survey web address, survey completion instructions, along with confidentiality of survey response assurances were provided directly to Datron employees in sealed envelopes from the consultant. All raw data and the employee ID log were kept in the consultant's office. Only summary results have been provided to Datron.

Data analyses focused on percentages within each level of multiple choices for participants overall and were then broken down by different employee groups. The employee group determinations were made by Datron's Employee Engagement Department. The groups are listed below:

- ALL   all employees
- SS   senior staff
- MT   management team
- SV   supervisors
- RD   research and development (engineering)
- DP   direct production
- AD   administrative staff
- ELL   English language learners (those who utilized translators for survey completion)

Open-ended items were analyzed looking for trends in responses and summaries, and where significant trends in participant responses were found, those trends were included in the key findings.

Second language learners were provided with translation services if they requested language support. Fifty-three employees requested language support. Language support was provided for Spanish, Vietnamese, Laotian, and Tagalog-Philippines employees.

While the survey was designed as the only data collection instrument, a small number (fifteen) of short directed follow-up interviews were conducted in order to clarify responses to an open-ended survey question related to "Group Most Difficult to Trust."

Findings and Recommendations

The evaluation findings are very clear: the vast majority of participants found the training valuable and their understanding of Datron's commitment to servant leadership increased substantially. Many of the participants expressed their appreciation for the experience. It is very clear that employees know how much the CEO cares about them and wants Datron and its employees to be successful.

Key Findings

- Substantial increases in understanding about servant leadership at Datron and for the interpersonal skills presented in levels 1 and 2. Greatest increase in effective listening skills.

- In terms of what participants have been able to implement in their lives, more effective listening was the most reported followed by taking more time to think about how to respond to others (think about your thinking).

- Employees across all analysis categories expressed concern about being judged on their servant leadership behavior and about how to manage on-time delivery goals with servant leadership.

Issues of Concern:

- Management groups were most often mentioned as the MOST DIFFICULT to trust. Within the explanations, all levels of management made some appearance, but the most striking finding was the explanations for the answer was similar across all management levels – that is actions inconsistent with what they say. A second group of explanations focused on communication up and down the management ladder.

- While in this study, overall percentages were high for increases in understanding or agreement with items related to rating the training or perceived support for the training, an analysis of group(s) with the highest "Disagree" and "Disagree + Moderately Disagree" percentages found one particular group ranked highest in the "Disagree" categories for half of the items analyzed. This is clear evidence of a systematic issue that should be explored.

Level 3 Training Recommendations

Objective for Level 3 Training: Bridge the concepts presented in levels 1 and 2 with concrete, articulated behaviors and expectations in order to increase organizational trust.

- Best Practices Development clearly linking servant leadership, interpersonal skills, and behaviors.
- Differentiated training – focused on job functions / teams / department. Reduce training sessions to 1 or 1 ½ hour. Use Level 3 training as a guide for on-going internal organizational learning.
- Begin development of self-evaluation protocols for individuals / teams / departments.

Summary of Findings for the Datron Servant Leadership Evaluation

In response to the question *What group do you find MOST DIFFICULT to trust at Datron? Why?* the management group was most often mentioned as the MOST DIFFICULT. Within the explanations, all levels of management made some appearance; but the most striking finding was the explanations for the answer was similar across all management levels – that is behaviors inconsistent with what they say. A second group of explanations focused on communication up and down the management ladder. Some commented on the CEO's transparency with business information, but felt that other information or behaviors were missing, very inconsistent, or not representative of servant leadership. Anger issues of some upper management members and/or inconsistent behavior depending on mood were also mentioned.

Several comments were made as to how the inconsistency in behavior often resulted in others being less willing to work on their own behaviors.

In response to the question *What did you find LEAST VALUABLE about your servant leadership training?* more than 80 percent of the responses in this category report there was nothing least valuable for them. They found the training very useful and many voiced appreciation for the training. While the second category of responses is much, much smaller, it is very important. Second language learners found the training not as valuable as it might have been for them due to language difficulties. Explanations included frustration with not being able to understand as much as they wanted and disappointment in not being able to gain as much as some of their coworkers.

There is substantial evidence that employees across all groups are concerned about being criticized regarding their servant leadership behavior. Changing behavior and learning new skills takes time and often changes are very subtle and not overtly discernable. The question becomes how does Datron encourage trying new skills and make room for employees to have numerous opportunities to practice and sometimes fail without criticism?

Research on change, as well as leadership development and organizational change, show that in order to sustain organization change both ongoing support and consistent opportunities to practice and develop new skills is essential. Most successful change is seen in programs with simultaneous top-down and bottom-up approaches. For Datron's servant leadership focus, this is apparent in servant leadership training for all employees (bottom-up) and the emphasis on transparency from the management staff (top-down). In addition, the Kellogg Foundation evaluation of outcomes and impact for leadership programs found that it took *a minimum of five years for the effects of leadership training to be readily apparent in organizations.* This is not to say that no change occurs before five years, but only that readily apparent organizational effects take longer to become easily discernible or institutionalized.

Change takes time and an important research finding is that changes in attitude do not always occur before behavior changes. Work with teacher professional development programs suggests that teachers are not willing or able to make wholesale changes in behavior/teaching strategies or their attitude after professional development training but rather make small, incremental changes in their teaching and classroom strategies. As teachers incorporate new teaching strategies and see positive changes in student outcomes/attitudes/performance, they are more likely to continue implementing new strategies in their classrooms. This continuous cycle of change, coupled with positive results provides a powerful source of reinforcement for continued growth and attitude change. As participants continue to practice and develop new skills and behaviors, they often deepen their understanding of the value of the new behaviors and attitudes.

Given these points, it is recommended that level 3 training include (but not limited) the following:

• Activities that continue to reinforce levels 1 and 3 learning.
• Development of Datron Servant Leadership Best Practices.
• Change length of training sessions from three hours to one or one and a half hours.

Identify a method for providing English language learners with language support during training sessions. Not necessarily bringing translators in; language support could be provided by other employees. Use of Datron employees as language support would require attention to scheduling training sessions for employees with specific languages together.

It is proposed that including some initial development of self-evaluation (for institutionalizing servant leadership, departments, teams, management) be explored. Without a commitment to institutionalizing servant leadership practices change can be strong in year 1 and gone the next due to elimination of support or key advocates/resources or leaders – by institutionalizing the practice, all become leaders/advocates and change is supported.

Conclusion of Findings for the Datron Servant Leadership Evaluation

The evaluation findings are very clear: the vast majority of participants found the training valuable and their understanding of Datron's commitment to servant leadership increased substantially. The data collected for this study are somewhat unique in that approximately 95% of Datron employees had completed both levels of training so nearly all Datron employees were surveyed about their servant leadership training experience. In addition, the response rate of 95% is phenomenal despite the fact that the survey itself was very long (101 items) and most employees needed an average of 2+ hours to complete it.

Participants found level 1 and 2 training materials clear and easily understood. Content in levels 1 and 2 has prepared participants for the recommended work of level 3 training – that of constructing and extending their understanding of servant leadership best practices related directly to the context of their work at Datron.

Revisiting the evaluation questions delineated earlier in this report show there is evidence of substantial increases in understanding of the concepts and skills in levels 1 and 2 training. Additionally, participants provided numerous accounts of how they have incorporated what they learned into their everyday activities. While participants report beginning to use what they learned, many noted that it would have been helpful to have more real-life examples as a reference.

Participants' self-evaluation of their own servant leader qualities—being authentic, being vulnerable, being accepting of others, being present and being useful—indicated an average of 60 percent rated themselves in the highest category "aware, working on it, and confidence is improving." These qualities represent complex psychological styles and are not easily quantifiable.

Participants' understanding of the specific interpersonal skills presented in the training—issues related to trust, how to think about your thinking, and effective listening skills—increased substantially. It is important to note that the increase reported is for *understanding*, but is not for using the skills. Of these three sets of skills, the comments from participants regarding how their behavior had changed as a result of their training in effective listening skills appear to be where the participants reported the most changes. This is not unexpected as these skills are more easily identified and used than are the other two skills—thinking about your thinking and trust. Thinking about your thinking appears to be the concept that was most difficult for some, especially the second language learners. Changes to thinking and perceptions are difficult for many people and require shifts in cognitive style. It is not surprising that fewer comments were made about how behavior had changed in relation to this concept.

For understanding of the issues related to trust, the majority of participants "good understanding" rating is high. Participant comments related to trust are of some concern, especially regarding their perceptions of inconsistency in management behavior (comments referenced, to one degree or another, leads, supervisors, department managers, upper management, senior management, and the CEO). While this is an unintended or perhaps unexpected outcome, it provides a golden opportunity for modeling servant leadership in action. *By all management taking a good look at both individual behavior, as well as organizational management behavior, and working on improving "the walk," employees will see that the commitment to servant leadership is real and it is likely that organizational trust will improve significantly.*

A second prominent area of concern is that there is substantial evidence that employees across all groups are concerned about being criticized regarding their servant leadership behavior and about how to juggle both on-time commitment concerns with trying new strategies. Both of these concerns could be described as "rock and a hard place" situations. However, what the issue really represents is the need for Datron management and policies to reflect the position that even when difficult business concerns appear to come into conflict with servant leadership, there is a way to accommodate both. Servant leadership does not mean not making hard decisions, but it does require transparency in the decision-making process and clear explanations for decisions. This is not to say that this is an easy process. This is an excellent choice for best practices development. In addition, an obvious question is how does Datron encourage employees to try new skills and to make room for employees to have numerous opportunities to practice and, to sometimes fail, without criticism? Specifically, what does this look like in on-the-ground management practices?

In summary, the overall findings are very encouraging and servant leadership training was for most employees a very positive experience. In the point of fact, many of the participants expressed their appreciation for the experience. It is very clear that employees know how much the CEO cares about them and wants Datron and its employees to be successful. The future for servant leadership at Datron appears to be bright.

The History of the Servant Leadership Institute

I am often asked why we started the Servant Leadership Institute. We were encouraged by many from inside and outside our company to share our story and experiences of implementing servant leadership at our radio manufacturing company, Datron World Communications, Inc. The success we experienced after implementing servant leadership was beyond what we expected and the response from our employees, suppliers, and customers was amazing. People that knew us thought Datron was a great business case on the results servant leadership could generate. As you know from my story in this book, I did not become an advocate for servant leadership until late in my career. However, my desire to have a training/education group within the companies I worked came earlier in my career from my first employer, Disneyland.

I grew up in the small town of Tustin in Southern California. When I was in high school the coolest job you could get was working for Disneyland in Anaheim. I was eighteen years old when I finally started my dream job as a "sweeper." I was required to wear an all-white uniform with black shoes, used a small broom sweeper in one hand and a portable trash container in the other. My job was to keep my assigned area in the park as clean as possible. I was assigned to work in Fantasyland. I remember my first day on the job did not involve any time working in the park. It was spent at the Disney University attending their required training for new hires. The Disney University taught us about the Disney way, why they do what they do, how we were to dress while "on stage" (the Disney way of saying while working in sight of the public), what we would wear, how our hair would be cut, and how you would conduct yourself while in the public eye.

I never forgot the training I received at the Disney University. After my first year with Disneyland, I was required to return to the Disney University for a refresher course. This was an annual requirement that I always looked forward to. After I finished college, I left Disneyland to accept a position in leadership as the Accounting Manager for a small company in Irvine, California. Over the years, I would be promoted into higher leadership positions and always had a desire to provide training similar to what I experienced. When I would budget for training, I would always dream about a "university" just like the one at Disneyland that invested their time and talents training employees like me. In my corporate career, prior to servant leadership, the training budget was always the first expense to be reviewed, reduced and, at times, completely eliminated. Later in life, I would start to realize that training was actually an investment in someone else's life. The desire was there to invest in others but I didn't get serious about starting a university-type training center until I worked at Datron World Communications.

I started working for Datron in October 1997 as the vice

president of finance, and within two years became the VP of finance and operations. The human resources department was part of my organization and in 2000, I started talking to our manager of human resources about starting a Datron University. My idea was based on what I had experienced at Disney University. I wanted to provide training for employees to help them with their work. I also wanted to include some life training, such as financial management, retirement planning, and health education for our employees. We spent several years talking about it, did some planning, and held one or two classes/courses, but never really got it off the ground until I was able to purchase Datron from my employer in 2004.

It was April 2003 when I was first exposed to servant leadership after meeting Ken Blanchard at my church. Ken was invited to speak on leadership at what we called the Spring Series. We invited special guest speakers each month that spring to teach different subjects to those in attendance. I met Ken personally when he spoke on a Wednesday night. During his talk, he challenged me to be a servant leader. In fact, he told me if I really believed what I believe then being a servant leader was not an option. I started my own journey in servant leadership that night. By the end of the year, I had a plan on paper to create a servant leader department within Datron. In November of 2004, I was able to purchase Datron from my employer and started the journey of leading a company with servant leadership principles. After buying the company, we immediately began changing the culture of the company. Datron was established as a company in 1971, so it already had a culture—one that had been under the power or positional leadership model for years. I first changed the mission and purpose of the company with the help of Jeanne McGuire, an organizational consultant. She has worked with me at Datron on our servant leadership culture since 2004. She helped the senior team develop our mission and purpose as well as our core values. In 2005, we started the journey of changing the culture of the company and planned to establish the Datron

University. In late 2005, we had made some progress. I wasn't comfortable yet calling servant leadership, servant leadership. Nor was I comfortable about sharing my faith with the leadership team, or even letting the team know why I was so dedicated to servant leadership. I finally decided that I had to let the leadership team know why I was doing what I was doing, and to let them know it was my faith that was driving my belief in servant leadership. I also decided to share with them that my faith was personal to me, that I had not been put in the CEO position at Datron to convert them to my faith, or require them to be religious. Our values, mission, and purpose at Datron require us to have a heart to help people and to do it the right way. That requirement continues today, Datron looks for people that have a desire to serve others.

In March 2008, I hired Tony Baron to work part-time (a minimum of ten hours per week) in our servant leadership department at Datron World Communications. He continued to pastor his small church in Oceanside, which remained his primary job. I had met Tony several years earlier when he became one of my spiritual advisors. At the time he and I met, I was under the spiritual authority of Pastor Shawn Mitchell at my home church, New Venture Christian Fellowship. Tony became an additional spiritual advisor for me, augmenting my spiritual learning at New Venture. Most of Tony's career prior to his ministry work was spent in the consulting world helping organizations with workplace violence prevention, in which he has extensive knowledge and is considered a subject matter expert.

The Servant Leadership Institute was formed in 2008, as a for-profit corporation in the State of California. I was the founder of the Institute and held the president and CEO title at startup and have held the CEO position to this day. Funding for the Institute comes from Lori (my wife) and myself. We believe servant leadership is our calling and you can't delegate your calling to others or ask others to fund it; your calling is your responsibility. Tony Baron was president of the Institute from March 2009 to November 2012. His primary function as president was teaching and writing. I remained the CEO with overall strategic and operational responsibility for the Institute. Tony continued his role as pastor with his church and also became active in leadership within the Anglican Church in North America. John Goehring, the CFO at Datron, was the Institute's CFO and Lori Barter, my wife, was the secretary. At the time Tony joined us, Datron had been on its servant leadership journey for four years. During his tenure as our president, we allowed him to focus on his gifts of teaching and writing. As an employee of Datron and commissioned by Lori and me, Tony wrote *The Art of Servant Leadership* based on hours of interviews he conducted with me documenting the Datron story and my transformation journey as the corporate leader. After *The Art of Servant Leadership* was released, we agreed to have Tony, again as a Datron employee, write a spiritual version about servant leadership called *The Cross and the Towel.*

We had our first Servant Leadership Conference in 2010, at a hotel on Harbor Island in San Diego. At the time, I was a member of an organization called the Chief Executive Network (CEN), a group of senior leaders in industry helping each other through the challenges of running both public and private companies. I really liked the approach they took to their conferences: no more than one-and-a-half days in length, focused on content and relationships, and they always ended on time. I decided to model the SLI conference after those I had experienced at CEN. I also believed that leaders learn best from speakers that focused on telling real-life stories of changes made in their companies which created the largest impact on inspiring others to change while at the same time achieving amazing results. We decided our conferences would focus on other people and not ourselves. We have consistently sold out each and every year since we started. In 2015, I was able to convince John Maxwell, Ken Blanchard, and Stephen M. R. Covey to attend and speak at our conference at the same time. We learned just before the conference that these three leadership thought leaders had never been on the stage together at the same time. History in the making! What a great time we had together that year; and most importantly, we inspired and equipped a record number of attendees.

In November 2013, Robin Swift became our general manager after Tony Baron resigned to take a full-time teaching position at Azusa Pacific University. Robin had joined the Institute in October 2011, as our director of client services. In February 2016, Robin became the president of the Institute.

The Servant Leadership Institute chose to focus on helping leaders implement servant leadership. We develop content around this topic and share our experiences (both personal and professional) on what it takes to transform yourself and your organization to focus on serving others. I have been very fortunate to have Ken Blanchard and John Maxwell as mentors through my own transformation, and recently over the past several years to have Stephen M. R. Covey in my life. Stephen and I have worked together teaching servant leadership through The Speed of Trust.

The Institute has always taken pride (OK, I know that is not a good servant leadership trait) in working with our clients to develop programs that work for them within their own organization. We believe that any organization that takes on changing its culture needs to be self-sustaining, not dependent on individuals or organizations outside of their company. In 2014, we worked with a client to develop a Lunch and Learn program for them to teach the "Nine Behaviors of a Servant Leader" to a core group of sixty leaders. We first helped in developing what we like to call Behavior Subject Experts (BSE). A BSE was selected to teach each of the servant leadership behaviors. We developed curriculum that includes slide decks and teaching workbooks for one hour lunch sessions where they could focus on each behavior over several weeks. We supported and trained each BSE. The program was a success and continues today.

In 2015, we were asked to be a partner with the City of Carlsbad in developing and participating in the Carlsbad Student Leadership Academy (CSLA), a program for high school students to learn about themselves in three modules: You School, focused on helping them with their own identification and finding their gifts; Lead School, focused on teaching servant leadership behaviors; and Serve School, focused on giving back to their community and helping others around them. The program is completely funded by the City of Carlsbad. It is exciting to be working with future leaders and teaching them about living their lives for the sake of others.

At our 2018 conference, we will be announcing a change to the Institute. We have decided to add a non-profit organization named the Servant Leadership Foundation. The Servant Leadership Institute will continue as a for-profit entity. All of the content generated since the inception of the Institute will be available for use and teaching by either organization. Our hope is that with the appropriate level of funding, we will be able to conduct research in servant leadership and teaching methods, develop training materials targeted for the multi-generations in the workplace today, and bring together like-minded people with the desire to change the world through servant leadership. We are excited about this change as it will allow us to pursue grants related to servant leadership research, development, and training.

At Datron, we invested in and developed our own servant leadership training materials. We could not find material on servant leadership implementation that we felt would be effective in our multi-cultural, international radio manufacturing company environment. Lori and I invested close to five hundred thousand developing a training program for servant leadership that included three modules of fifteen hours each. We also decided that the servant leadership training at Datron should be given to all employees. We developed groups of fifteen to twenty people and began the training in 2007. We developed module one that focuses on individual transformation and then module two which focuses on team transformation. After the second module, we hired a consultant from Berkeley, who specialized in evaluating educational programs and their effectiveness, to develop a survey to seek input from our employees regarding the effectiveness of the first two modules. It was also used to determine what module three should include while focusing on implementing what was learned in the first two modules. I've included some information about the survey and its results in the appendix for you. Each employee at Datron has gone through forty-five hours of servant leadership training. In 2016, we developed a refresher course for our employees and concluded the refresher training with all of our employees in 2017.

Based on what we learned from our internal servant leadership training, we developed the Nine Behaviors of a Servant Leader. These nine behaviors generated the most significant transformation in our organization and our employees' lives. We teach the Nine Behaviors of a Servant Leader to help others transform into servant leaders. We have also included in the appendix, the introduction, and first chapter of *The Servant Leadership Journal*. The journal was written to take you on an eighteen-week journey to transform you and your organization.

We continue to believe we are called to develop content and teach servant leadership implementation, to share our knowledge about the transformation you will go through, the change in your leadership behaviors that will be required, and how others will perceive you and your journey. Our goal is to inspire and equip you to change your leadership mindset to one that is focused on service, not self. The Servant Leadership Institute and the Servant Leadership Foundation are here to serve you.

Our hope is these two organizations will continue the work of training and developing servant leaders well after Lori and I are gone from this earth. You will notice that our name is not part of either of these two organizations. We believe that Servant Leadership is greater than any one individual. We committed from the first day we started on this journey that our name would not be part of the organization. We believe this to be the best succession plan for what the Institute and Foundation are called to do.

Servant Leadership Journal

(Sample Introduction and Chapter 1)

Welcome to the *Servant Leadership Journal*. The purpose of this journal is to help you change your leadership behaviors. I personally like to look at leadership from a servant's perspective, with a focus on servant leadership—but don't let the word "servant" keep you from making the most important change you'll ever make in your leadership beliefs.

I was a product of the corporate power model. After graduating from college in 1979, I entered into training in the command-and-control corporate world. I embraced the command-and-control leadership model and, in fact, made it the most important priority in my life. At the young age of twenty-four, I was put into my first management role, and at twenty-five, I was pushed into the senior finance role in my division with the title of "controller." I had a real desire to succeed in life. Because I was driving a company car, had a senior leadership role in a company, and was empowered to direct the actions of others, I thought I had arrived. I embraced my new title with all my heart, but the only trouble was, my heart was nowhere to be found in most of my decisions as a leader. Don't get me wrong; at the time, I believed I was a great leader. From that point forward, I literally sacrificed everything in my life for success.

When I was challenged in my leadership beliefs by Ken Blanchard in 2003, I was ready for a change. I had just been burned again by my employer and was tired of giving my all to a corporate world that didn't care about me or my family.

Sound familiar? At the time of this writing, the engagement level of the workforce in the U.S. is at an all-time low of 30 percent. In addition, Gallup does an annual poll that surveys the confidence we have in our country's institutions. Congress is last on the list (no surprise here) with the lowest confidence level—less than 10 percent—and the confidence level for corporations runs at about 25 percent. I recently heard a senior leader in the survey industry say we are a country of very lonely individuals.

As Ken Blanchard, John Maxwell, and most of the other experts in the field teach, leadership is all about influence. I started looking at and changing my leadership beliefs in 2004. Change is a funny thing. It sounds great and looks good, but it feels like…well, you fill in the blank. In my case, I had to face the reality that changing my behaviors was the only way I could convince those I influenced that I was serious about changing the way I lead others, that I really cared.

"Walk the talk" was a very popular catch phrase during that time, but most of the leaders who were saying it didn't really believe in it. Or maybe they believed in it, but they didn't understand it. They thought if they got out of their office and walked around on a regular basis, that meant they were walking their talk. I worked in a company where the CEO literally scheduled a time once every week to walk around the company. The employees loved it; they knew that at the same time each week he would come around and say hi to them. Mind you, he didn't pay them very well, they were never allowed to participate in the company's bonus program and their medical benefits were no better than standard. The company had no mission or purpose, nor was there a culture with any type of collective collaboration. In that company, I reported to a division president. Over the first five years of my tenure with that company, I worked for four different division presidents.

I believe leaders need to back up their talk with behaviors. I found a conceptual paper recently that proposes a very telling definition of destructive leadership behavior, along with a descriptive model. The authors defined destructive leadership behavior as: "The systematic and repeated behavior by a leader, supervisor, or manager that violates the legitimate interest of the organization by undermining and/or sabotaging the organization's goals, tasks, resources, and effectiveness and/or the motivation, well-being, or job satisfaction of his/her subordinates."[11]

As you think about this definition, keep in mind that we have the lowest engagement of U.S. workers in our nation's history. The good news is, this can change if we as leaders are willing to change. I believe we can. I started the Servant Leadership Institute in 2010 after I had spent six years implementing servant leadership in the radio company I had purchased in 2004. As we were starting our journey of change at Datron, we searched for training material or programs that were available in the marketplace to help us implement servant leadership in our company. In the end, we decided to create our own training program for our employees. We developed three training modules of fifteen hours each, totaling forty-five hours of training for every employee in our radio company. Through the experiences we gained during that process, along with feedback from our employees, we developed the Nine Behaviors of a Servant Leader. We believe these behaviors are key to becoming a better leader—one who focuses on others first and would like to see all destructive leadership behavior eliminated.

One of the tools I used to change my own behavior was journaling. Every couple days, I would spend time writing about my experiences, feelings, challenges, and goals. This led to a better understanding of where I wanted to go. Sometimes I would write down ideas, sometimes goals, and sometimes just thoughts. That time of journaling and reflection provided the basis for the change I wanted to make in my leadership behaviors.

---

11 Ståle Einarsen, Merethe Schanke Aasland, Anders Skogstad, "Destructive leadership behavior: A definition and conceptual model," The Leadership Quarterly, Vol. 18 (2007), pg. 207–216.

Today, I want to pass this tool on to you. This journal will allow you to walk through the nine behaviors I feel are so key to becoming a servant leader. Let's change that old, worn out saying, "Walk the Talk" to "Behave your Talk."™ Show others you are serious about becoming a different type of leader—one who can be trusted to act the same as your talk, one who really cares. **We are on this journey together.** Dedicate time to walk through these behaviors. I believe there are four distinct steps for you to take in your journey with each behavior:

- **Educate yourself on the meaning of each behavior.** Use Google, Wikipedia or whatever you need to gain an understanding of what the behavior means.

- **Understand where you are on each behavior.** Be realistic in your review; ask others, including your spouse, to tell you how you behave. Be courageous to see the real you.

- **Apply what you are learning to your life.** What specific areas do you want to improve in? What specific traits related to each behavior do you what to change? Set daily goals to affect that change.

- **Reflect.** Record the results of your journey—what you've learned about yourself, what others have noticed, how you feel about the change you are making, and what else you would like to do to continue your journey in each behavior.

Once you have completed this cycle, start it all over again for as long as it takes to change each behavior.

A word of caution: Your old behaviors are hard to eliminate. The longer you've been trained in the command-and-control power world, the longer it will take to change those behaviors. And another word of caution: Know that when you are under pressure and the stress level in your life increases, those old behaviors will show themselves. That's okay. Recognize it, apologize for it, journal about it, and get better. It is not the end of the world. Trust me; I know this part of the transformation better than I would like to admit.

You've already started the journey; now start writing. When I first started journaling, it was not comfortable for me, nor was it easy. Changing our behaviors is not easy, but it is possible. Join me on this journey and make our world a better place.

I'm on this journey with you every step of the way!

1

Intentional Servant Leadership

"The world is waiting for us to graduate from ourselves."
—Shannon L. Alder

My wife, Lori, is my best friend. She loves for me to have coffee ready for her when she gets up in the morning. I don't know why and it really isn't required that I understand why; I desire to make her happy unconditionally. The first thing I do after getting up each morning is make her a fresh pot of coffee. She takes care of me and all my needs. More importantly, she makes our house our home. When she travels and I stay home with our two cats, Juno and Wiley, the heart of our home is missing. Lori is the best daily example I have of a servant leader. She takes care of our kids, cats, home, and me in an unbelievable way. She serves her family with all her heart and soul, so making her coffee brings me as much joy as it does her.

Serving first sounds easy; however, when our life unfolds each day and we are faced with challenges, our motives are challenged. Your motives need be pure, which is not always easy for most of us. I believe you can transform both your mindset and motives to serve first; it doesn't have to come naturally. The most important measure of serving others is this: Are those you come in contact with better off after they have come in contact with you? This may be easy to accomplish with those we meet for a single moment in time on the streets, in stores, or in our community. But what about those we love—our families, spouse, children—or those we spend most of our waking hours with at work? How do we keep our motives pure in serving others? We need to graduate from ourselves. I love this quote from Booker T. Washington: "Those who are happiest are those who do the most for others." When we serve others with a pure heart, we have joy in our lives.

Author Mollie Marti puts it this way: "The more you become aware of and respond to the needs of others, the richer your own life becomes." We should not only serve others; we also need to develop a sense of awareness of their needs before we serve them. Poet and author Harley King raises the bar even higher, saying, "Service to others in their time of need is a privilege and an honor." Albert Einstein said it best: "The high destiny of the individual is to serve rather than to rule."

It's time to start your journaling process. The four steps of transformation we taught in Chapter 1 are what we recommend you use in the next thirty days.

There is no magic amount of time to spend on each of the four areas. This is your journey, your transformation, and you are in control of the speed at which you journal. We have provided enough pages for fourteen days of journaling. I will caution you, based on my experience in my journaling, don't rush it. If you have someone you trust, I suggest you share with them what you are learning about yourself and your journey in the behaviors of servant leaders. Start with the learning process. Take some time to study what it means to serve. Then take what you've learned and make sure you understand how it might apply to your own life. Once you feel you have an idea of what you would like to accomplish, initiate some goals you want to accomplish in your day-to-day life. Then leave room to reflect on the results you experience in your journey.

Spend time every day in your journal. It may feel uncomfortable at first, but stick with it. Those you influence will start to see a difference in how you behave. Record the challenges you face so you can look back at some time in the future to see your progress.

Now, pick up a pen and get started. Remember, I'm on this journey with you.

DAY 1

What I've learned today about serving first:

How might what I've learned apply to my life?

What will I do tomorrow to serve someone?

Reflection:

DAY 2

What did I learn from my reflection yesterday about serving first? Did I learn anything new about serving first that I want to add?

How might what I've learned apply to my life?

What will I do tomorrow to serve someone?

Reflection:

DAY 3

What did I learn from my reflection yesterday about serving first? Did I learn anything new about serving first that I want to add?

How might what I've learned apply to my life?

What will I do tomorrow to serve someone?

Reflection:

DAY 4

What did I learn from my reflection yesterday about serving first? Did I learn anything new about serving first that I want to add?

How might what I've learned apply to my life?

What will I do tomorrow to serve someone?

Reflection:

"Truly caring is truly liberating."
—Farmer Able in *Farmer Able*, by Art Barter

DAY 5

What did I learn from my reflection yesterday about serving first? Did I learn anything new about serving first that I want to add?

How might what I've learned apply to my life?

What will I do tomorrow to serve someone?

Reflection:

DAY 6

What did I learn from my reflection yesterday about serving first? Did I learn anything new about serving first that I want to add?

How might what I've learned apply to my life?

What will I do tomorrow to serve someone?

Reflection:

DAY 7

What did I learn from my reflection yesterday about serving first? Did I learn anything new about serving first that I want to add?

How might what I've learned apply to my life?

What will I do tomorrow to serve someone?

Reflection:

"If you're not making someone else's life better, then you're wasting your time. Your life will become better by making other lives better."
—Will Smith

DAY 8

What did I learn from my reflection yesterday about serving first? Did I learn anything new about serving first that I want to add?

How might what I've learned apply to my life?

What will I do tomorrow to serve someone?

Reflection:

DAY 9

What did I learn from my reflection yesterday about serving first? Did I learn anything new about serving first that I want to add?

How might what I've learned apply to my life?

What will I do tomorrow to serve someone?

Reflection:

DAY 10

What did I learn from my reflection yesterday about serving first? Did I learn anything new about serving first that I want to add?

How might what I've learned apply to my life?

What will I do tomorrow to serve someone?

Reflection:

DAY 11

What did I learn from my reflection yesterday about serving first? Did I learn anything new about serving first that I want to add?

How might what I've learned apply to my life?

What will I do tomorrow to serve someone?

Reflection:

DAY 12

What did I learn from my reflection yesterday about serving first? Did I learn anything new about serving first that I want to add?

How might what I've learned apply to my life?

What will I do tomorrow to serve someone?

Reflection:

> *"Doing nothing for others is the undoing of ourselves."*
> —Horace Mann

DAY 13

What did I learn from my reflection yesterday about serving first? Did I learn anything new about serving first that I want to add?

How might what I've learned apply to my life?

What will I do tomorrow to serve someone?

Reflection:

DAY 14

What did I learn from my reflection yesterday about serving first? Did I learn anything new about serving first that I want to add?

How might what I've learned apply to my life?

What will I do tomorrow to serve someone?

Reflection:

You made it! Remember, everyone transforms their behaviors at different rates. Keep that in mind if you are working through this process with others in your organization; this is a transformational journal for you. Don't compare your progress to others.

One of the best tools I was taught while learning to change my behaviors was a visualization exercise. It is a process whereby you identify something you do each day that will remind you of the behavior. Like me, you will feel like a fool the first time you do this. I would encourage you to go through the visualization exercise I've included at the end of each chapter. It is well worth your time and will have a lasting impression on your life.

Your Visualization Exercise—Serving First

The visualization of serving first in my life is making a pot of coffee for my wife Lori as soon as I get up in the morning. Close your eyes and picture what serving first means to you. This will be the picture that will represent serving first for you. Make sure it is a picture of something you do every day. It may include serving a person in your family or in your organization. Make sure it is something you do each and every day.

Write your true life visualization of what serving first means to you.

Congratulations on completing your first behavior of servant leadership. Keep up the great work!

Made in the USA
Monee, IL
26 January 2021